Teacher Supplement to

Bible Stories for All Without the Dogma

A Part of Cultural Literacy

Kenneth E. Walsh

Reading comprehension, vocabulary development, essay writing, discussion questions, assessment quizzes

Copyright 2020 © by Kenneth E. Walsh

All rights reserved, including the right to distribute, transmit, scan, copy, or reproduce any portion of this book.

No part of this book may be distributed, transmitted, scanned, copied, or reproduced without the author's permission.

Send requests for permissions to kenwalsh3@icloud.com.

Discounted bulk orders for *Bible Stories for All without the Dogma* and orders for the teacher supplement may be ordered directly by emailing your request to the author at kenwalsh3@icloud.com.

Direct quotes or quotes with minor modifications from the Good News Bible, Today's English ©American Bible Society, 1992, use the Good News Translation® (Today's English Version, Second Edition) © 1992 American Bible Society. All rights reserved.

Bible text from the Good News Translation (GNT) is not to be reproduced in copies or otherwise by any means except as permitted in writing by American Bible Society, 1865 Broadway, New York, NY 10023 (www.americanbible.org).
GNT

Library of Congress Control Number: 2020902526

ISBN: 978-0-9991565-7-5

Cover picture: Courtesy of pixabay.com.

Summit Crossroads Press
Columbia, Maryland 21045

About the Teacher Supplement of
Bible Stories for All without the Dogma

Because writing styles and customs change over time, the Bible stories of old are summarized in today's language along with a few choice passages that are timeless and touching.

The worksheets may be used in an academic setting to guide students through the reading or to ensure they have read the chapter on their own or to help the student focus on the key facts. In a non-academic setting, such as a Sunday church school or youth discussion group, you might consider using the worksheets for an oral review or team competition.

The section in each chapter, entitled "Questions for Consideration/Discussion," is useful for group discussion or written assignment. They supplement the fact-based worksheets with deeper thinking questions that often do not have a single answer. They provide an opportunity for students to share and then discuss their different perspectives. Ideally, they will learn from each other and develop deeper thoughts.

Several chapters include a few student activities for your consideration.

At the end of several chapters there is a quiz that may be used in an academic setting or as an oral review or competitive game in youth groups.

You may reproduce the worksheets, quizzes, and crossword puzzles with permission for classroom use or youth group discussion.

Table of Contents

- Chronology 3
- Chapter 1: Background: Who are we? 4
- Chapter 2: Introduction 8
- Chapter 3: Geography – Civilizations, Topography & Seasons 10
- Chapter 4: Roads 19
- Chapter 5: Bible Organization 21
- Chapter 6: Introduction to the Book of Genesis 32
- Chapter 7: Creation Part One - Seven Days 34
- Chapter 8: Creation Part Two: Adam & Eve 36
- Chapter 9: Cain & Abel 45
- Chapter 10: Noah & the Flood 48
- Chapter 11: Tower of Babel 51
- Chapter 12: Abraham's Journeys 58
- Chapter 13: Abraham's Sons 62
- Chapter 15: Isaac 73
- Chapter 16: Isaac & Jacob 75
- Chapter 17: Jacob 80
- Chapter 18: Joseph & His Brothers 89
- Chapter 19: Joseph & the Wife of the Captain of the Palace Guard 93
- Chapter 20: Joseph Interprets Dreams & Becomes Governor of Egypt 95
- Chapter 21: Joseph's Brothers Go to Egypt & Return There with Benjamin 97
- Chapter 22: The Missing Cup and Joseph Identifies Himself 102
- Chapter 23: Jacob's Family Moves to Egypt & Famine Strikes Harder 105
- Chapter 24: Jacob's Last Request, Blessing, and Death 107
- Chapter 25: Moses' Early Life 120

Chapter 26: The Ten Plagues 126

Chapter 27: The Ten Commandments 128

Chapter 28: Joshua 139

Chapter 29: Judges 141

Chapter 30: Ruth 143

Chapter 31: Samuel 151

Chapter 32: Saul 157

Chapter 33: Young David 160

Chapter 34: David's Reign 165

Chapter 35: David's Sons 170

Chapter 36: Solomon 173

Chapter 37: Esther 187

Vocabulary 192

Chronology

BCE

Prehistory	Creation stories, Cain & Abel and Noah
1800-1700	Patriarchs in Canaan (Abraham, Isaac, Jacob)
1700-1250	Israelites in Egypt (Jacob through Joseph)
1250	Exodus (Moses)
1220-1200	Conquest of the Promised Land (Joshua)
1200-1030	Period of the Judges
1100	Ruth
1030-1010	Saul
1010-970	David
970-931	Solomon
950	Queen of Sheba's visit
931	Solomon dies. Two kingdoms form as Israel and Judah.
721	Fall of Israel. Exile.
587	Fall of Judah. Exile.
331	Return to Israel.

Source: Who's Who in the Bible, Joan Comay. 1971, p. 16-18.

Name: _____   Date _____

Chapter 1: Background: Who are we?

1. Name the types of humans and one interesting fact about each one.

   a. _____

   b. _____

   c. _____

   d. _____

   e. _____

   f. _____

2. How would you define a hunter-gatherer?

   _____

   _____

3. How did hunter-gatherers change during the Agricultural Revolution?

   _____

   _____

4. Since farmers could produce more food than was needed, what did some people do?

   _____

   _____

5. Why did ancient societies have polytheistic practices?

   _____

   _____

Name: _____   Date _____

Chapter 1: Background: Who are we?

1. Name the types of humans and one interesting fact about each one.

   Australopithecine – lived over 3 million years ago, believed to be an ancestor of humans, walked upright, had a brain 1/3 the size of ours.

   a. **Homo habilis – used simple tools, such as stone chips to scrape animal hides and cut meat. They had brains half the size of ours.**

   b. **Homo erectus – learned to control fire and communicate using language. They used a "3-in-1" tool called the stone axe to butcher meat, dig out root crops, and cut wood.**

   c. **Homo Sapiens – developed more sophisticated tools, such as fish hooks, bows and arrows, spears, and sewing needles. They created art, music, rituals, and social networks. Exchanged resources over large areas.**

   d. **Homo Sapiens: Neanderthals – had brains the size of ours. They cared for their sick and injured. They may have believed in an afterlife.**

   e. **Homo Sapiens: Cro-Magnons – made cave paintings and small statues of humans.**

2. How would you define a hunter-gatherer?

   A hunter-gatherer lived by hunting animals and gathering wild food (e.g., wild cereal (e.g., wheat, oats, and rice), fruit, nuts.)

3. How did hunter-gatherers change during the Agricultural Revolution?

   As hunter-gatherers began to domesticate or train wild animals and plants, they were able to settle in one place and take advantage of a steadier supply of food.

4. Since farmers could produce more food than was needed, what did some people do?
   Since farming involving domesticated plants and animals could produce more food than needed, some people began to specialize (e.g., as weavers, toolmakers, potters.)

5. Why did ancient societies have polytheistic practices?
   They attributed the forces of nature, such as flooding, pestilence, and drought, to different gods who needed to be pleased to avoid these unpleasant events.

Crossword Puzzle Chapter 1

ACROSS:
5. Belief in many gods
7. Large animal similar in appearance to a buffalo
8. Train wild animals & plants
9. Explain or give credit
10. Large extinct mammal with a trunk and long hair

DOWN:
1. Life after death
2. Swiftly spreading disease
3. Insulting
4. Long spell of dry weather
6. Belief in one God

Crossword Puzzle Chapter 1

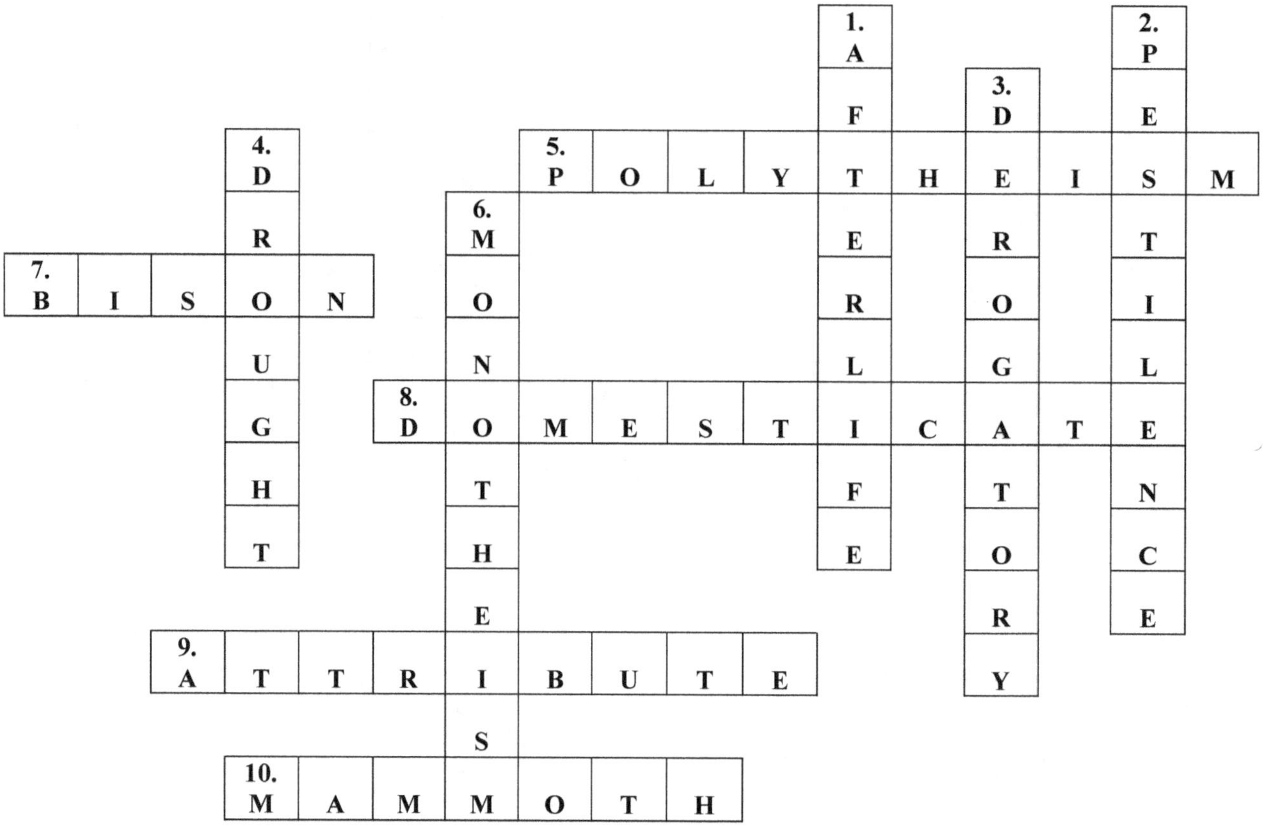

1. A F T E R L I F E
2. P E S T I L E N C E
3. D E R O G A T O R Y
4. D R O U G H T
5. P O L Y T H E I S M
6. M O N O T H E I S M
7. B I S O N
8. D O M E S T I C A T E
9. A T T R I B U T E
10. M A M M O T H

ACROSS:

5. Belief in many gods
7. Large animal similar in appearance to a buffalo
8. Train wild animals & plants
9. Explain or give credit
10. Large extinct mammal with a trunk and long hair

DOWN:

1. Life after death
2. Swiftly spreading disease
3. Insulting
4. Long spell of dry weather
6. Belief in one God

Name: _____   Date _____

Chapter 2: Introduction

1. What did ancient Mesopotamians and Egyptians believe happened after they died?
   _____

2. Why were many people polytheistic?
   _____
   _____

3. What did the believers in polytheism have to do?
   _____

4. How was the Israelites' new faith different than the polytheistic believers?
   _____
   _____

5. Why do people study the Bible?
   _____
   _____
   _____
   _____

Name: _____   Date _____

Chapter 2: Introduction

1. What did ancient Mesopotamians and Egyptians believe happened after they died?
   They believed in a life after death.

2. Why were many people polytheistic?
   Polytheism, a belief in many gods, offered an explanation as to why bad things happened (e.g., floods, drought, pestilence, earthquakes, volcanoes, disease, etc.)

3. What did the believers in polytheism have to do?
   They had to please the gods usually by making burnt offerings of animals and crops.

4. How was the Israelites' new faith different than the polytheistic believers?
   The Israelites believed in one God who was separate from the universe. He was a loving God who was concerned about the poor and downtrodden.

5. Why do people study the Bible?
   We study the Bible to better understand Western culture, to develop ourselves spiritually, and to learn from the successes and failures of others. We study the Bible because it has influenced people for thousands of years. It is reflected in our culture, language, history, politics, art, music, and literature.

Chapter 3: Geography – Civilizations, Topography & Seasons

Supplemental Consideration and/or Discussion Questions

1. In ancient times would you prefer to be a herder or a farmer? If you were one of the few who specialized, what craft would you practice (e.g., weaver, toolmaker, potter, etc.)?

2. Where would you want to live in ancient times? In terms of topography, rainfall, and temperature?

3. If you were an ancient settler in Israel which topographical zone would you want to live in?

Name: _____   Date _____

Chapter 3: Geography – Civilizations, Topography & Seasons

1. What is geography?
   _____

2. When were the prehistoric times?
   _____

3. What does CE Mean? _____

4. How else is CE sometimes expressed? _____

5. Who developed the world's first systems of writing and what were they called? Why did they develop them?

   _____

   _____

6. Who developed an organized set of laws and what was it called?
   _____

7. What type of religion did ancient Mesopotamians and Egyptians practice and what did they believe?
   _____

(Over)

8. List the four topographical zones in Israel.

   a. _____

   b. _____

   c. _____

   d. _____

9. List Israel's two seasons and when they occur.

   a. _____

   b. _____

10. Explain the rainfall pattern in Israel. Compare Israel's rainfall to Baltimore-Washington.

    _____
    _____
    _____
    _____
    _____

11. Explain why Jerusalem has mild summer temperatures while there are scorching temperatures in most of the Middle East.

    _____
    _____
    _____
    _____
    _____
    _____
    _____
    _____
    _____

Name: _____   Date _____

Chapter 3: Geography – Civilizations, Topography & Seasons

1. What is geography?
   Geography is the study of the earth's physical features and its cultural features.

2. When were the prehistoric times?
   Prehistoric times are the times before the development of writing in 3,000 BCE.

3. What does CE Mean? **Common Era**

4. How else is CE sometimes expressed? **A.D./AD – In the year of the Lord**

5. Who developed the world's first systems of writing and what were they called? Why did they develop them?
   The Sumerians in Mesopotamia developed the world's first systems of writing called pictograph and later cuneiform to facilitate trade with a system of written records.

6. Who developed an organized set of laws and what was it called?
   King Hammurabi. The Code of Hammurabi.

7. What type of religion did ancient Mesopotamians and Egyptians practice and what did they believe?
   They practiced polytheism, a belief in many gods.

(Over)

8. List the four topographical zones in Israel.
    a. **Coastal Plain**
    b. **Central Mountains**
    c. **Jordan Valley**
    d. **Transjordanian Mountains**

9. List Israel's two seasons and when they occur.
    a. **Dry Season – summer**
    b. **Rainy/Wet Season – winter**

10. Explain the rainfall pattern in Israel. Compare Israel's rainfall to Baltimore-Washington.
    Winds bring moisture from the Mediterranean Sea to Israel. Rainfall diminishes as the wind moves inland and especially over the mountains. In normal years Israel receives 12-16" in the coastal and Central Mountain areas. By comparison the Baltimore-Washington area averages 41 inches of rain annually.

11. Explain why Jerusalem has mild summer temperatures while there are scorching temperatures in most of the Middle East.
    On a typical summer day, temperatures begin to climb immediately after sunrise. A short time later a cooling sea breeze begins to blow in from the Mediterranean Sea. The cool sea breeze reaches Jerusalem in the Central Mountains about noon and keeps the capital's temperature in the comfortable mid-80s. However, the temperatures in the Transjordanian Mountains soar into the low 100s. What is left of the cool sea breeze only reaches there in the late afternoon by which time the breeze is too little and too late to have a cooling effect.

Crossword Puzzle Chapters 2-3

ACROSS:
4. One of 600 wedge-shaped characters in Sumerian writing
7. Period before the development of writing in 3000 BCE
9. Physical features of the earth

DOWN:
1. A rectangular, stepped tower with an altar at the top
2. Study of the physical & cultural features of an area
3. An organized set of laws
5. Supplying dry lands with water by canals & pipes
6. Observable event
8. Religious group

Crossword Puzzle Chapters 2-3

ACROSS:
4. One of 600 wedge-shaped characters in Sumerian writing
7. Period before the development of writing in 3000 BCE
9. Physical features of the earth

DOWN:
1. A rectangular, stepped tower with an altar at the top
2. Study of the physical & cultural features of an area
3. An organized set of laws
5. Supplying dry lands with water by canals & pipes
6. Observable event
8. Religious group

Crossword Puzzle Chapter 3

ACROSS:
2. A triangle-shaped area of land made of soil deposited by a river
4. A long, thin reed; paper-like writing material
5. Productive
7. Egyptian writing form
8. Departure
9. Peoples of southwest Asia

DOWN:
1. A terrible shortage of food that can cause starvation
3. Farming
6. Gradual development from a simple to a more complex form

17

Crossword Puzzle Chapter 3

			1. F				2. D	E	L	T	3. A		
			A								G		
			M				4. P	A	P	Y	R	U	S
5. F	E	R	T	I	L	6. E					A		
			N			V					R		
		7. H	I	E	R	O	G	L	Y	P	H	I	C	S
						L					A		
		8. E	X	O	D	U	S				N		
						T							
		9. S	E	M	I	T	I	C					
						O							
						N							

ACROSS:
2. A triangle-shaped area of land made of soil deposited by a river
4. A long, thin reed; paper-like writing material
5. Productive
7. Egyptian writing form
8. Departure
9. Peoples of southwest Asia

DOWN:
1. A terrible shortage of food that can cause starvation
3. Farming
6. Gradual development from a simple to a more complex form

Name: _____ Date _____

Chapter 4: Roads

1. List two examples of topography influencing the location of roads.

    a. _____

    b. _____

2. What are the advantages and disadvantages of rainfall on travel in ancient times?

    a. Advantages: _____

    _____

    b. Disadvantages: _____

    _____

3. Which season was preferred for traveling? _____

4. Compare the road building tasks of the ancient times and the Roman times.

    a. Ancient Times

        i. _____
        ii. _____
        iii. _____
        iv. _____

    b. Roman Times

        i. _____
        ii. _____
        iii. _____
        iv. _____

5. How did people travel long distances in ancient times? _____

6. What were donkeys used for?

    _____

Name: _____   Date _____

Chapter 4: Roads

1. List two examples of topography influencing the location of roads.
   a. **Near the Mediterranean Sea roads followed the coastline where the land was flat and easy to walk.**
   b. **In the Transjordanian Mountains roads generally followed the flat mountain ridges.**

2. What are the advantages and disadvantages of rainfall on travel in ancient times?
   a. **Advantages: Some rainfall is needed to provide water for (drinking) wells and for food to eat (crops).**
   b. **Disadvantages: Too much rain caused roads to be muddy or flooded in low-lying areas.**

3. Which season was preferred for traveling? **The dry, summer season**

4. Compare the road building tasks of the ancient times and the Roman times.
   a. **Ancient Times:**
      i. **Cut down trees**
      ii. **Push boulders and stones aside**
      iii. **Use shallow fords to cross river beds**
      iv. **Use switchbacks along slopes**
   b. **Roman Times**
      i. **Level the road surface by flattening out hills and filling in valleys**
      ii. **Use flat stones as the road surface**
      iii. **Hold the road surface in place with curbing**
      iv. **Plan for drainage with curbs and cut-outs to move water away from the roads to prevent erosion and washouts.**

5. How did people travel long distances in ancient times? **By walking**

6. What were donkeys used for? **To transport goods**

Chapter 5: Bible Organization

Supplemental Notes

1. Introduction: The Bible contains many different forms of writing: prose, poetry, hymns, prayers, and codes of law. It was originally written on scrolls known as biblia in Greek.

2. Three sections:

    a. The Law (Torah) or the Five Books of Moses: Genesis, Exodus, Leviticus, Numbers, and Deuteronomy also known as the Pentateuch (or five scrolls).

    b. The Prophets (Nevi'im) including the early prophets: Joshua, Judges, Samuel, and Kings. And later prophets including Isiah, Jeremiah, Ezekiel, and the Twelve Minor Prophets.

    c. The Writings (Ketuvim) including the Psalms, Proverbs, the Book of Job, the Book of Daniel, and the Book of Chronicles.

3. Timeline Periods:
    - Prehistory: Creation through the Tower of Babel
    - Early Israelite Leaders (The Patriarchs: Abraham, Isaac, and Jacob; and Joseph)
    - Egypt, Moses, and Exodus
    - The Promised Land: Joshua, Judges, and Ruth
    - Kingdoms of Israel (Samuel, Saul, David, and Solomon)
    - Exile & Return
    - Jesus
    - The Early Christians

Name: _____   Date _____

Chapter 5: Bible Organization

1. What does ta biblia mean? How does it relate to the Bible?

   _____

   _____

2. The Bible is divided into two parts: _____ and _____

3. Testament means _____ or _____

4. What is the Old Testament about?

   _____

   _____

5. What was the Old Testament originally called? (Hint: by the Jewish people before there were Christians?) _____ or _____

6. Some of the Old Testament books were written hundreds of years after the events they describe. How were they passed down through the generations?

   _____

7. What is the New Testament about?

   _____

   _____

Name: _____   Date _____

Chapter 5: Bible Organization

1. What does ta biblia mean? How does it relate to the Bible?
   Ta biblia means the books. The word Bible comes from ta biblia. The Bible is a collection of 66 books by more than 40 authors.

2. The Bible is divided into two parts: **The Old Testament** and **the New Testament**.

3. Testament means **covenant** or **a solemn agreement between two parties**.

4. What is the Old Testament about?
   The Old Testament is the story of the Israelites during the time before Jesus (BC or BCE) and their unique faith in one God.

5. What was the Old Testament originally called? (Hint: by the Jewish people before there were Christians?) **The Holy Scripture or Tanak**

6. Some of the Old Testament books were written hundreds of years after the events they describe. How were they passed down through the generations? **By oral tradition**

7. What is the New Testament about?
   The New Testament tells the story of Jesus, the early Christians, and their new faith in one God and salvation through Jesus.

Crossword Puzzle Chapters 4-5

ACROSS:
1. Letter
3. Church law
5. Religious writing
7. A switchback road for climbing a steep grade
11. A house for a religious order; e.g., monks
12. The hoped-for person who would free the Israelites

DOWN:
2. Familiar saying
4. Prediction
6. Covenant
8. A solemn agreement between two parties
9. Banishment; required to leave one's homeland
10. A place where a stream may be crossed by wading

Crossword Puzzle Chapters 4-5

		1.E	2.P	I	S	T	L	E						
			R											
3.C	A	N	O	N										
			V											
			E				4.P							
5.S	C	R	I	P	T	6.U	R	E						
	B					E	O							
						S	P							
		7.S	W	I	T	C	H	B	A	8.C	K			
						A	E			O			9.E	
	10.F					M	S			V			X	
11.M	O	N	A	S	T	E	R	Y		12.M	E	S	S	I	A	H
	R					N				N			L	
	D					T				A			E	
										N				
										T				

ACROSS:
1. Letter
3. Church law
5. Religious writing
7. A switchback road for climbing a steep grade
11. A house for a religious order; e.g., monks
12. The hoped-for person who would free the Israelites

DOWN:
2. Familiar saying
4. Prediction
6. Covenant
8. A solemn agreement between two parties
9. Banishment; required to leave one's homeland
10. A place where a stream may be crossed by wading

Name: _____   Date _____

Chapters 1-5: Overview Quiz

1. Define hunter-gatherer?
   _____
   _____

2. How did hunter-gatherers change during the Agricultural Revolution?
   _____
   _____

3. Since farmers could produce more food than was needed, what did some people do?
   _____
   _____

4. Why did ancient societies have polytheistic practices?
   _____
   _____

5. What did ancient Mesopotamians and Egyptians believed happened after they died?
   _____

6. Why were many people polytheistic?
   _____
   _____

7. What did the believers in polytheism have to do?
   _____
   _____

(Over)

8. How was the Israelites' new faith different than the polytheistic believers?

   _____

   _____

9. Define geography?

   _____

10. When are prehistoric times?

    _____

11. What does CE Mean? _____

12. What type of religion did ancient Mesopotamians and Egyptians practice and what did they believe?

    _____

13. List the four topographical zones in Israel.
    - a. _____
    - b. _____
    - c. _____
    - d. _____

14. List Israel's two seasons and when they occur.

    a. _____ - _____   b. _____ - _____

15. What are the advantages and disadvantages of rainfall on travel in ancient times?
    a. Advantages: _____

       _____

    b. Disadvantages: _____

       _____

(Over)

16. Which season was preferred for traveling? _____

17. How did people travel long distances in ancient times? _____

18. What were donkeys used for? _____

19. The Bible is divided into two parts: _____ and _____.

20. Testament means _____ or _____.

21. What is the Old Testament about?
_____
_____

22. What was the Old Testament originally called? (Hint: by the Jewish people before there were Christians?) _____

23. Some of the Old Testament books were written hundreds of years after the events they describe. How were they passed down through the generations?
_____

24. What is the New Testament about?
_____
_____

I have neither given nor received any assistance on this quiz.

_____
Signature   Date

Name: _____   Date _____

Chapters 1-5: Overview Quiz

1. Define hunter-gatherer?
   A hunter-gatherer lived by hunting animals and gathering wild food (e.g., plants, berries, nuts, etc.)

2. How did hunter-gatherers change during the Agricultural Revolution?
   As hunter-gatherers began to domesticate or train wild animals and plants, they were able to settle in one place and take advantage of a steadier supply of food.

3. Since farmers could produce more food than was needed, what did some people do?
   Since farming involving domesticated plants and animals could produce more food than needed, some people began to specialize (e.g., as weavers, toolmakers, potters, etc.).

4. Why did ancient societies have polytheistic practices?
   They attributed the forces of nature, such as flooding, pestilence, and drought, to different gods who needed to be pleased in order to avoid these unpleasant events.

5. What did ancient Mesopotamians and Egyptians believed happened after they died?
   They believed in a life after death.

6. Why were many people polytheistic?
   Polytheism, a belief in many gods, offered an explanation as to why bad things happened (e.g., floods, pestilence, drought, earthquakes, volcanoes, disease, etc.).

7. What did the believers in polytheism have to do?
   They had to please the gods usually by making burnt offerings of animals and crops.
   (Over)

8. How was the Israelites' new faith different than the polytheistic believers?

    The Israelites believed in one God who was separate from the universe. He was a loving God who was concerned about the poor and downtrodden.

9. Define geography?

    Geography is the study of the earth's physical features and its cultural features.

10. When are prehistoric times?

    Prehistoric times are the times before the development of writing.

11. What does CE Mean? **The Common Era**

12. What type of religion did ancient Mesopotamians and Egyptians practice and what did they believe?

    They practiced polytheism, a belief in many gods.

13. List the four topographical zones in Israel.
    a. **Coastal Plain**
    b. **Central Mountains**
    c. **Jordan Valley**
    d. **Transjordanian Mountains**

14. List Israel's two seasons and when they occur.

    a. Dry Season – summer   b. Rainy/Wet Season – winter

15. What are the advantages and disadvantages of rainfall on travel in ancient times?
    c. **Advantages: Some rainfall is needed to provide water for (drinking) wells and for food to eat (crops).**
    d. **Disadvantages: Too much rain caused roads to be muddy or flooded in low-lying areas.**

(Over)

16. Which season was preferred for traveling? **The dry, summer season**

17. How did people travel long distances in ancient times? **By walking**

18. What were donkeys used for? **To transport goods**

19. The Bible is divided into two parts: **The Old Testament** and **the New Testament**.

20. Testament means **covenant** or **a solemn agreement between two parties**.

21. What is the Old Testament about?

    The Old testament is the story of the Israelites during the time before Jesus (BC or BCE) and their unique faith in one God.

22. What was the Old Testament originally called? (Hint: by the Jewish people before there were Christians?) **The Holy Scripture or Tanak**

23. Some of the Old Testament books were written hundreds of years after the events they describe. How were they passed down through the generations? **By oral tradition**

24. What is the New Testament about?

    The New Testament tells the story of Jesus, the early Christians, and their new faith in one God and salvation through Jesus.

    I have neither given nor received any assistance on this quiz.

    _____
    Signature   Date

Name: _____   Date: _____

Chapter 6: Introduction to the Book of Genesis

Introduction

1. Genesis means _____

2. Genesis can be divided into two main parts:

    a. _____

    b. _____

3. List three aspects of the Babylonian and Jewish religious views of the world.

    Babylonian View   Jewish View

    a. _____   a. _____

    b. _____   b. _____

    c. _____   c. _____

Name: _____   Date: _____

Chapter 6: Introduction to the Book of Genesis

Introduction

1. Genesis means **origin or beginning.**

2. Genesis can be divided into two main parts:
    a. **Creation stories**
    b. **Patriarch stories**

3. List three aspects of the Babylonian and Jewish religious views of the world.

    Babylonian View   Jewish View

    a. Polytheism   **a. Monotheism**

    b. Selfish gods   **b. Loving God**

    c. The gods are part of the universe.   **c. God is separate from the universe.**

    d. Humans exist to serve the gods   **d. Humans are made in God's image.**

Name: _____   Date: _____

Chapter 7: Creation Part One - Seven Days

1. What was God's first command in creating the world?

   _____

2. What did God create on each of the first six days?

Day	What God created:
One	_____
Two	_____
Three	_____
Four	_____
Five	_____
Six	_____

3. After God created the human beings on the sixth day, what did God think of creation?

   _____

4. What did God do on the seventh day?

   _____

Name: _____   Date: _____

Chapter 7: Creation Part One - Seven Days

1. What was God's first command in creating the world? (Genesis 1:3)

    Let there be light. (Gen 1:3) (GNT)

2. What did God create on each of the first six days? (Genesis 1:3-30)

Day	What God created:
One	**Light**
Two	**Water and sky**
Three	**Dry land and plants**
Four	**Specific light: sun, moon, and stars**
Five	**Water creatures and birds**
Six	**Animals and humans**

3. After God created the human beings on the sixth day, what did God think of creation? (Genesis 1:31)

    God was very pleased.

4. What did God do on the seventh day? (Genesis 2:3)

    He/she stopped working. He/she rested.

Chapter 8: Creation Part Two: Adam & Eve

Supplemental Student Activity

1. Should God have punished Adam, Eve, and the snake? Was God fair? Analyze your answer. Hold a debate or conduct a trial on guilt and/or punishment. Reaction?
    a. Who is the most guilty? The least? Why?
    b. Who lied?
    c. What are their motives?
    d. How does each have a responsibility to the other?
    e. How do they ignore their responsibilities? *Shirking responsibility/pass blame*
    f. Do we need rules? *E.g., Sports/games/traffic.*

Name: _____   Date: _____

Chapter 8: Creation Part Two: Adam & Eve

1. Where did God put man? _____

2. What does Eden mean? _____

3. What command did God give man when God placed him in the garden? What would happen if the man disobeyed the command?
   _____

4. What did the snake tempt the woman to do?
   _____

5. How did the snake convince Eve to eat from the tree of knowledge?
   _____

6. When they heard the sound of God in the garden, what did they do? _____

7. What did God do to the snake who tempted the woman?
   _____

8. What was the woman's punishment?
   _____

9. What was the man's punishment?
   _____

Name: _____   Date: _____

Chapter 8: Creation Part Two: Adam & Eve

1. Where did God put man? (Gen 2:8) **In the garden in Eden**

2. What does Eden mean? **delight or garden of God**

2. What command did God give man when God placed him in the garden? What would happen if the man disobeyed the command? (Gen 2:16-17)
   Not to eat the fruit from the tree of knowledge; man would die the same day

3. What did the snake tempt the woman to do? (Gen 3: 1-5)
   To eat the fruit from the tree

4. How did the snake convince Eve to eat from the tree of knowledge? (Gen 3:1-5)
   He told her that she would "be like God and know what is good and what is bad." (Gen 3:5) (GNT)

5. When they heard the sound of God in the garden, what did they do? (Gen 3: 8) **They hid.**

6. What did God do to the snake who tempted the woman? (Gen 3:14)
   He made the snake crawl on its belly and eat dust as long as it lived.

7. What was the woman's punishment? (Gen 3:16)
   She had increased trouble in pregnancy and increased pain in giving birth.

8. What was the man's punishment (Gen 3:17-19)
   The ground would be under a curse. He would have to work hard all his life to grow enough food for you.

Crossword Puzzle Chapters 6-8

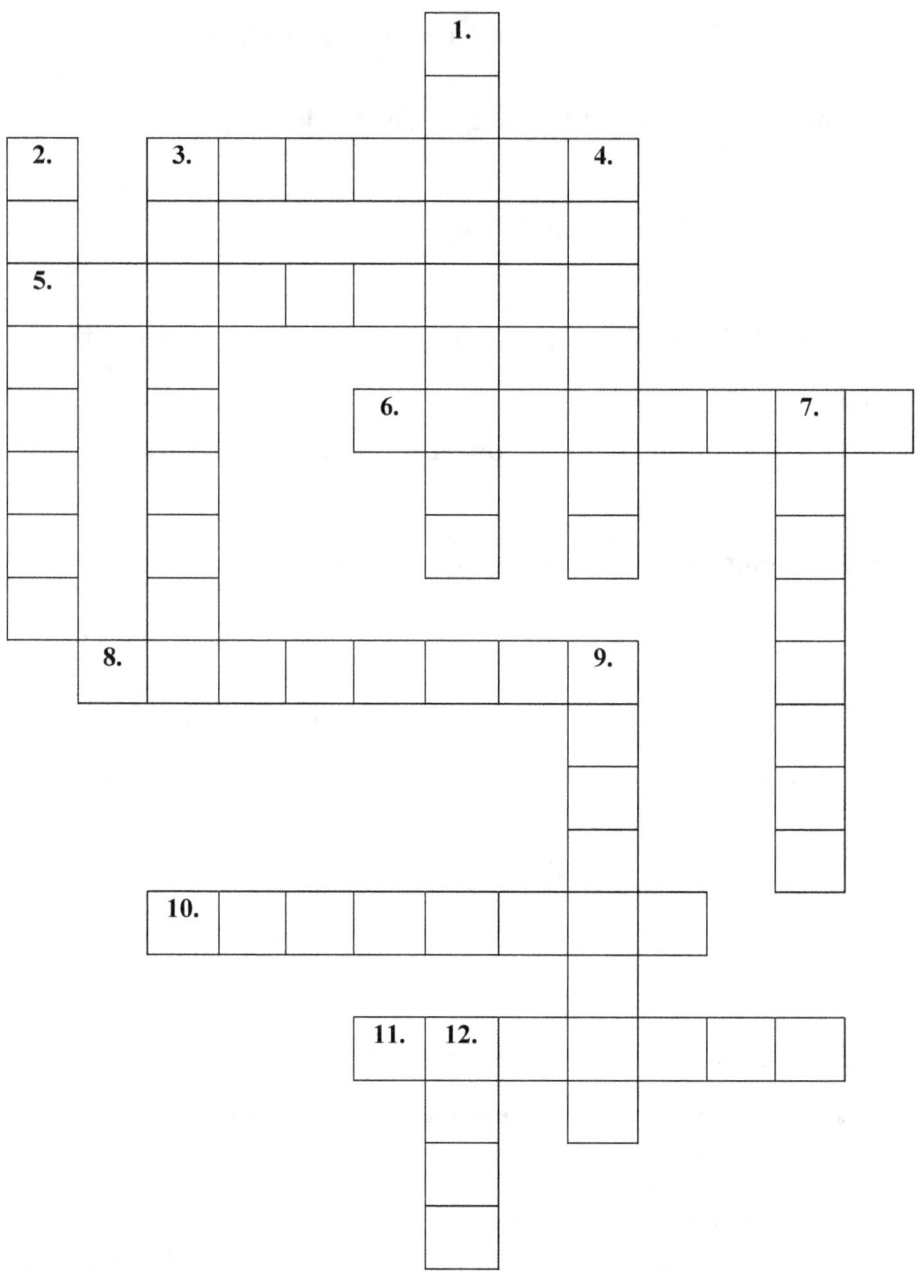

ACROSS:
3. In a confused, unorganized state
5. To be saved; i.e., for everlasting life
6. Handmade object
8. Deserted
10. External openings of the nasal cavity
11. Origin, beginning

DOWN:
1. Respected founder
2. Be like
3. Prepare for farming or growth
4. Tricky; sly
7. Misfortune
9. Enclosed
12. Delight or garden of God

Crossword Puzzle Chapters 6-8

			1.P			
			A			
2.R	3.C	H	A	O	T	I	C	4.C
E	U			R		U
5.S	A	L	V	A	T	I	O	N
E	T			A		N
M	I		6.A	R	T	I	F	A	C	7.T
B	V		C		N		A
L	A		H		G		L
E	T						A
	8.D	E	S	O	L	A	T	9.E		M
						N		I
						G		T
						U		Y
	10.N	O	S	T	R	I	L	S
						F
		11.G	12.E	N	E	S	I	S
			D		D
			E
			N

ACROSS:
3. In a confused, unorganized state
5. A confused, unorganized state
6. Handmade object
8. Deserted
10. External openings of the nasal cavity
11. Origin, beginning

DOWN:
1. Respected founder
2. Be like
3. To grow crops
4. Tricky; sly
7. Misfortune
9. Enclosed
12. Delight or garden of God

Name: _____   Date: _____

Chapters 6-8: Creation Quiz

Read each question carefully. Fill in the blank or circle the letter that best answers the question.

1. Genesis means _____

2. The Book of Genesis is divided into two parts:
    a. _____
    b. _____

3. What was God's first command in creating the world?
    a. "Let there be a dome to divide the water."
    b. "Let lights appear in the sky to separate day from night."
    c. "Let there be light."
    d. "Let the water be filled with many kinds of living beings."

4. After God created the human beings on the sixth day, what did God think of creation?
   _____

5. Eden means _____

6. What were the unusual tree in the Garden of Eden?
    a. knowledge and life   c. fruit trees
    b. oaks   d. pines

7. How did the snake convince Eve to eat from the tree of knowledge?
    a. that she will live forever
    b. that she would be like God and know what is good and what is bad
    c. that she will have power over Adam
    d. that she will have power over the creatures

(Over)

41

8. What did God do to the snake that tempted the woman?
   a. declared the snake to be Satan
   b. required the snake to reproduce
   c. empowered the snake to tempt mankind
   d. made the snake crawl on its belly and eat dust

9. What was the woman's punishment?
   a. assist the snake
   b. cultivate crops
   c. stay in the Garden of Eden for the rest of her life
   d. increase her pain in giving birth

10. What was the man's punishment?
    a. to forever have to hunt snakes
    b. to work hard all his life
    c. to have to stay naked
    d. to stay in the Garden of Eden

11. Patriarch means:
    a. respected founder
    b. governor
    c. church law
    d. prediction

I have not received nor provided any assistance on this quiz.

_____

Signature   Date

Name: _____   Date: _____

Chapters 6-8: Creation Quiz

Read each question carefully. Fill in the blank or circle the letter that best answers the question.

1. Genesis means **origin or beginning (creation)**

2. The Book of Genesis is divided into two parts:
    a. **Creation stories**
    b. **Patriarchs stories**

3. What was God's first command in creating the world?
    a. "Let there be a dome to divide the water."
    b. "Let lights appear in the sky to separate day from night."
    c. "Let there be light."
    d. "Let the water be filled with many kinds of living beings."

4. After God created the human beings on the sixth day, what did God think of creation? **He/she rested.**

5. Eden means **delight of garden of God**

6. What were the unusual tree in the Garden of Eden?
    a. **trees that give knowledge**   c. fruit trees
    b. oaks   d. pines

7. How did the snake convince Eve to eat from the tree of knowledge?
    a. that she will live forever
    b. that she would be like God and know what is good and what is bad
    c. that she will have power over Adam
    d. that she will have power over the creatures

(Over)

8. What did God do to the snake that tempted the woman?
   a. declared the snake to be Satan
   b. required the snake to reproduce
   c. empowered the snake to tempt mankind
   d. made the snake crawl on its belly and eat dust

9. What was the woman's punishment?
   a. assist the snake
   b. cultivate crops
   c. stay in the Garden of Eden for the rest of her life
   d. increase her pain in giving birth

10. What was the man's punishment?
    a. to forever have to hunt snakes
    b. to work hard all his life
    c. to have to stay naked
    d. to stay in the Garden of Eden

11. Patriarch means:
    a. respected founder
    b. governor
    c. church law
    d. prediction

I have not received nor provided any assistance on this quiz.

_____

Signature   Date

Chapter 9: Cain & Abel

Supplemental Student Activity

1. Responsibility for Special Relations – Keeping the Bond:

    Can you imagine giving your best friend a birthday gift and he or she just gives it back to you, rejecting your kindness? Cain may have felt the same hurt. What do you do in this situation?

    Possible answer: Ask your best friend what is the matter. Although you are insulted and perhaps publicly humiliated, if you are truly a friend, you are there for him/her when he/she does something out of the ordinary. You can always react but, before you act in kind, you may want to give him/her the option of explaining and possibly apologizing. Maybe something just happened in his/her family such as a death or serious illness, and he/she is lashing out in a distraught manner. Maybe unbeknownst to you, someone has belittled the type of gift you gave and he/she, in a weak moment, went along with the crowd for a regrettable putdown of your gift. Perhaps your question will make him/her aware of how painful his/her rejection was to you, and he/she will offer you a heartfelt apology. But being there for others, especially in a close relationship like best friends or spouses, is a key responsibility that is hard to do but often deeply appreciated.

Name: _____   Date _____

Chapter 9: Cain & Abel

1. What were the names of Adam and Eve's two sons?

   _____   _____

2. What were the occupations of these two sons? _____

   _____

3. Whose offering did God reject? _____

4. Who killed whom? _____

5. What did Cain say to God about his brother?

   _____

6. What did God do to Cain? _____

   _____

7. How did God protect Cain? _____

   _____

8. What was the name of Adam and Eve's third son?

   _____

Name: _____   Date _____

Chapter 9: Cain & Abel

1. What were the names of Adam and Eve's two sons? (Gen 4:1-2)
   Cain and Abel

2. What were the occupations of these two sons? (Gen 4:2)
   Cain was a farmer and Abel a shepherd

3. Whose offering did God reject? (Gen 4:5) **Cain's**

4. Who killed whom? (Gen 4:8) **Cain killed Abel**

5. What did Cain say to God about his brother? (Gen 4:9)
   "I don't know. Am I supposed to take care of my brother?" (Gen 4:9) (GNT)

6. What did God do to Cain? (Gen 4:11-12)
   Placed him under a curse so he could no longer farm. He will be a homeless wanderer.

7. How did God protect Cain? (Gen 4:15)
   By putting a mark on Cain to warn anyone he met not to kill him

8. What was the name of Adam and Eve's third son? (Gen 4:25) **Seth**

Chapter 10: Noah & the Flood

Supplemental Note

1. Flood stories were part of many ancient cultures (e.g., Egyptian, Greek, Hindu, Chinese, Mexican, and Native American). Enter "flood legends" in a search engine for more details.

Supplemental Consideration/Discussion

1. After the flood Noah offered a gift of thanks to God. How do you give thanks? For example, when someone helps you, how do you respond?

Name: _____   Date _____

Chapter 10: Noah & the Flood

1. Why was God sorry?
   _____

2. Why did God decide to save Noah?
   _____

3. How many animals was Noah to take into the Ark?
   _____

4. How long did the rain fall on the earth? _____

5. What bird did Noah send out first? _____

6. Noah then sent out another bird three times, each time a week apart. What happened to this bird each time? What kind of bird was it?
   _____
   _____
   _____

7. What did Noah do after he and his family and the animals left the ark?
   _____

8. What covenant/promise did God make with Noah and his family?
   _____

9. What sign did God give to Noah as a symbol of his covenant?
   _____

Name: _____   Date _____

Chapter 10: Noah & the Flood

1. Why was God sorry? (Gen 6:5-6)
   God was sorry because he/she saw how wicked everyone on earth had become.

2. Why did God decide to save Noah? (Gen 6:8-10)
   God was pleased with Noah. He had no faults and was the only good man of his time.

3. How many of each kind of animal was Noah to take into the Ark? (Gen 6:19-20)
   A male and a female of each kind of animal

4. How long did the rain fall on the earth? (Gen 7:4) **Forty days and forty nights**

5. What bird did Noah send out first? (Gen 8:7) **A raven; it did not come back**

6. Noah then sent out another bird three times, each time a week apart. What happened to this bird each time? What kind of bird was it? (Gen 8:8-12)
   Each time Noah sent a dove. The first time it returned since it did not find a place to land. The second time it returned with an olive twig. The third time it did not return. Noah knew dry ground was reappearing again.

7. What did Noah do after he and his family and the animals left the ark? (Gen 8:20)
   He offered a sacrifice to God for saving him and his family.

8. What covenant/promise did God make with Noah and his family? (Gen 8:21)
   To never destroy all living things because of what people do.

9. What sign did God give to Noah as a symbol of his covenant? (Gen 9:11-17)
   A rainbow

Chapter 11: Tower of Babel

Supplemental Student Activity
1. Build a model ziggurat with a stairway to "heaven" (to the altar table on top). Suggest dimensions no greater than 12" (L) x 8" (W) x 10" (H) so they can fit on most bookshelves. With 4 levels (steps).

Name: _____   Date _____

Chapter 11: Tower of Babel

1. What building material did the wanderers in the land of Babylon make?
   _____

2. What did they plan to build?
   _____

3. Why did they want to build these?
   _____
   _____
   _____

4. What did God do to prevent the people from continuing their work?
   _____
   _____

Name: _____   Date _____

Chapter 11: Tower of Babel

1. What building material did the farmers in the land of Babylon make? (Gen 11:3)

    They made bricks and baked them in the sun to harden them.

2. What did they plan to build? (Gen 11:4)

    A city and then a tower to reach the sky.

3. Why did they want to build these? (Gen 11:4)

    They wanted to draw people together in their city with its high tower stretching toward the heavens. They wanted to make a name for themselves and not be scattered all over.

4. What did God do to prevent the people from continuing their work? (Gen 11:7-8)

    God scattered them all over the earth and mixed up their language so they could not talk to each other in the same language.

Name: _____ Date: _____

Chapters 9-11: Cain & Abel, Noah & Tower of Babel Quiz

1. What was Cain's occupation?
   a. shepherd
   b. farmer
   c. musician
   d. toolmaker

2. Who said, "Am I supposed to take care of my brother?"
   a. Abel
   b. Cain
   c. Seth
   d. Adam

3. Who said: You are driving me off the land and away from your presence. I will be a homeless wanderer on the earth, and anyone who finds me will kill me."
   a. Abel
   b. Cain
   c. Seth
   d. Jubal

4. What did God do to Cain?
   a. thanked him for his gift
   b. helped him reap bountiful crops
   c. placed him under a curse and made him a homeless wanderer
   d. rejoiced in his goodness

5. For what was God sorry?
   a. for creating Eve because she disobeyed him
   b. for creating Adam because he was easily misled
   c. for putting people on earth because they were wicked
   d. for creating Cain because he killed Abel

6. What did God tell Noah that his covenant sign would be?
   a. serpent
   b. lamb
   c. burning bush
   d. rainbow

7. What did Noah do after he and his family and the animals left the ark?
   a. offered a sacrifice to God
   b. built a temple to God
   c. prayed to the gods
   d. thanked his family

(Over)

8. What did God do to prevent the people from continuing their work in Babylon?
   a. He mixed up their language.
   b. He scattered them.
   c. He/she turned them into stone.
   d. Both a & b.

9. Inherit means:
   a. to receive
   b. to raise animals
   c. take away
   d. grow crops

10. Ark
    a. short arm
    b. bug
    c. garden
    d. a huge boat

I have neither given nor received any assistance on this quiz.

_____

Signature   Date

Name: _____   Date: _____

Chapters 9-11: Cain & Abel, Noah & Tower of Babel Quiz

1. What was Cain's occupation?
   a. **shepherd**
   b. farmer
   c. musician
   d. toolmaker

2. Who said, "Am I supposed to take care of my brother?"
   a. Abel
   b. **Cain**
   c. Seth
   d. Adam

3. Who said: You are driving me off the land and away from your presence. I will be a homeless wanderer on the earth, and anyone who finds me will kill me."
   a. Abel
   b. **Cain**
   c. Seth
   d. Adam

4. What did God do to Cain?
   a. thanked him for his gift
   b. helped him reap bountiful crops
   c. **placed him under a curse and made him a homeless wanderer**
   d. rejoiced in his goodness

5. For what was God sorry?
   a. for creating Eve because she disobeyed him
   b. for creating Adam because he was easily misled
   c. **for putting people on earth because they were wicked**
   d. for creating Cain because he killed Abel

6. What did God tell Noah that his covenant sign would be?
   a. serpent
   b. lamb
   c. burning bush
   d. **rainbow**

7. What did Noah do after he and his family and the animals left the ark?
   a. **offered a sacrifice to God**
   b. built a temple to God
   c. prayed to the gods
   d. thanked his family

(Over)

8. What did God do to prevent the people from continuing their work in Babylon?
   a. He mixed up their language.
   b. He scattered them.
   c. He/she turned them into stone.
   d. Both a & b.

9. Inherit means:
   a. **to receive**
   b. to raise animals
   c. take away
   d. grow crops

10. Ark
    a. short arm
    b. bug
    c. garden
    d. a huge boat

I have neither given nor received any assistance on this quiz.

_____

Signature   Date

Name: _____   Date _____

Chapter 12: Abraham's Journeys

1. Which world religions trace their roots back to Abraham?

    a. _____
    b. _____
    c. _____

2. List the five places Abram lived. (Hint: One is a return place.)

    a. _____
    b. _____
    c. _____
    d. _____
    e. _____

3. Who moved with Abram to Canaan?

    a. _____
    b. _____

4. Why did Abram and Lot split up?

    _____

5. Where did they go?

    a. Lot went to _____
    b. Abram stayed _____

6. What caused trouble between Abram and Lot and their herdsmen?

    _____

(Over)

58

7. How did Abram settle the trouble?

   _____

   _____

8. Where did Lot settle with his family?

   _____

9. Where did Abram go?

   _____

10. What was the custom for making family decisions then? (See Commentary)

    _____

11. What were some of the advantages to Abram in letting his nephew have the first choice when Abram was entitled to the first choice by their customs?

    _____

    _____

    _____

Name: _____   Date _____

Chapter 12: Abraham's Journeys

1. Which world religions trace their roots back to Abraham?

    a. **Judaism**

    b. **Christianity**

    c. **Islam**

2. List the five places Abram lived. (Hint: One is a return place.)

    a. **Ur**

    b. **Haran**

    c. **Shechem, Canaan**

    d. **Egypt**

    e. **Canaan**

3. Who moved with Abram to Canaan? (Gen 12:5)

    a. **Sarai, his wife**

    b. **Lot, his nephew**

4. Why did Abram and Lot split up? (Gen 13:6)

    There was not enough pasture land for their two flocks.

5. Where did they go? (Gen 13:11-12)

    a. Lot went to **the Jordan Valley**

    b. Abram stayed **in the Central Mountain region of Canaan near Hebron.**

6. What caused trouble between Abram and Lot and their herdsmen? (Gen 13:5-7)

    There was limited pastureland for their flocks

    (Over)

7. How did Abram settle the trouble? (Gen 13:8-11)

   Abram proposed that they separate and gave Lot the first choice of land.

8. Where did Lot settle with his family? (Gen 13:12)

   Jordan Valley

9. Where did Abram go? (Gen 13:13)

   Central Mountain region of Canaan, near the town Hebron

10. What was the custom for making family decisions then? (See Consideration #4)

    It was the custom to defer to the elder in making family decisions.

11. What were some of the advantages to Abram in letting his nephew have the first choice when Abram was entitled to the first choice by their customs?

    There would be no more jealous feelings among Lot's tribe toward Abram's tribe regarding grazing. It would show Abram's love and respect for his nephew.

Chapter 13: Abraham's Sons

Supplemental Student Activity

1. Covenants are solemn agreements with mutual obligations. Consider doing a trust walk with pairs of students. One leads the other who is blindfolded. Try to pair up students who do not know each other well or are at least not friends. Have a few turns maybe around a desk and/or up a few stairs. Consider doing it without the students talking so the guided student is completely dependent on the guiding student. After a few minutes, have the students switch roles. At the end provide an opportunity for the students to express their feelings, perhaps of responsibility and dependency. Next, consider asking what agreements or understandings they have in their family (e.g., proving income, doing the shopping for food, making dinner, washing dishes, cleaning the house, walking the dog, taking out the trash, doing the laundry, etc.) Ask how they would feel if the person responsible does not fulfill the expectation. While we do not use the word covenant in our families, there are rules or agreements that keep things working well. Tie the discussion back to covenants and note how someone may feel if a covenant or solemn agreement is broken. A major theme in the Bible is one of covenants between God and the Israelites. This is the first of many others we will examine.

Name: _____ Date _____

Chapters 13-14: Abraham's Sons/ Abraham Told to Sacrifice Isaac

1. What did God promise Abram? _____

2. What was predicted in Abram's dream?

   _____
   _____
   _____
   _____

3. Who arranged for Hagar to have Abram's child? Why?

   _____

4. What was Hagar's attitude toward Sarai after Hagar became pregnant?

   _____

5. How did Sarai treat Hagar? What happened?

   _____

6. What did the angel promise Hagar?

   _____
   _____

7. Why did God rename Abram? _____

8. What was God's covenant with Abram?

   _____
   _____
   _____

(Over)

9. What was the physical sign of God's covenant with Abraham? _____

10. How old were Abraham and Sarah when God promised that they would have a child of their own? _____

11. What did Abraham do for the three travelers who approached his tent?

_____

_____

12. What did one of the travelers tell Abraham about his wife?

_____

13. What is the name of Sarah's son? _____

14. What did Sarah tell Abraham to do with Hagar and her son? Why?

_____

15. How did Abraham feel? Why?

_____

16. What was God's plan?

_____

17. What did God command Abraham to do with his son, Isaac?

_____

18. Why did God tell Abraham to sacrifice his son?

_____

Name: _____   Date _____

Chapters 13-14: Abraham's Sons/ Abraham Told to Sacrifice Isaac

1. What did God promise Abram? (Genesis 15:1, 4-5) **a son, many descendants.**

2. What was predicted in Abram's dream? (Genesis 15:13-15)
   Abram's descendants will be slaves in a foreign land for 400 years; God will punish the nation that enslaves Abram's descendants; Abram's descendants will take great wealth with them when they leave. God promises to give Abram's descendants the land from Egypt's border to the Euphrates River.

3. Who arranged for Hagar to have Abram's child? Why? (Genesis 16:2-3)
   In accordance with the customs of the time, Sarai told Abram to try to have a child with her slave. They had lived ten years in Canaan and still had no children.

4. What was Hagar's attitude toward Sarai after Hagar became pregnant? (Genesis 16:4)
   Hagar became proud and despised Sarai.

5. How did Sarai treat Hagar? What happened? (Genesis 16:6)
   Sarai treated Hagar so cruelly that Hagar ran away.

6. What did the angel promise Hagar? (Genesis 16:10)
   The angel promised Hagar many descendants. She mentioned that her son will live apart from his relatives.

7. What did God rename Abram? (Genesis 17:5) **Abraham.**

8. What was God's covenant with Abram? (Genesis 17:5)
   He/she commanded Abraham to obey God. Promised that Abram would be the ancestor of many nations, that he would have many descendants, that some of them will be kings.
(Over)

9. What was the physical sign of God's covenant with Abraham? (Genesis 17:13) **Circumcision.**

10. How old were Abraham and Sarah when God promised that they would have a child of their own? (Gen 17:17) **Abraham was 100; Sarah was 90.**

11. What did Abraham do for the three travelers who approached his tent? (Genesis 18:4)
    He gave them a place to rest under the shade of a nearby tree. He washed their dusty feet. He offered them food to replenish their strength.

12. What did one of the travelers tell Abraham about his wife? (Genesis 18:10)
    The traveler said that Sarah will have a son in nine months.

13. What is the name of Sarah's son? (Genesis 21:3) **Isaac**

14. What did Sarah tell Abraham to do with Hagar and her son? Why? (Genesis 21:10)
    She asked Abraham to send Hagar and Ishmael away so he could not inherit their wealth.

15. How did Abraham feel? Why? (Genesis 21:11)
    Abraham was quite troubled by her request because Ishmael was his first-born son.

16. What was God's plan? (Genesis 21:12-13)
    Abraham's descendants would be through Isaac, the son God had promised.

17. What did God command Abraham to do with his son, Isaac? (Gen 22:2)
    God commanded him to take Isaac to a mountain in Moriah and offer him as a sacrifice to God.

18. Why did God tell Abraham to sacrifice his son? (Gen 22:12)
    God was testing whether Abraham would honor and obey him.

Crossword Puzzle Chapters 9-14

ACROSS:
3. A male sheep
4. The act of pacifying or buying off
5. Cut off the foreskin of a penis
7. A woman who is not a wife, but holds a recognized position in the household
8. Having more than one wife or husband at a time

DOWN:
1. Receive as an heir
2. A friendly and generous reception
6. An angry, wrinkled facial expression
9. A huge boat

Crossword Puzzle Chapters 9-14

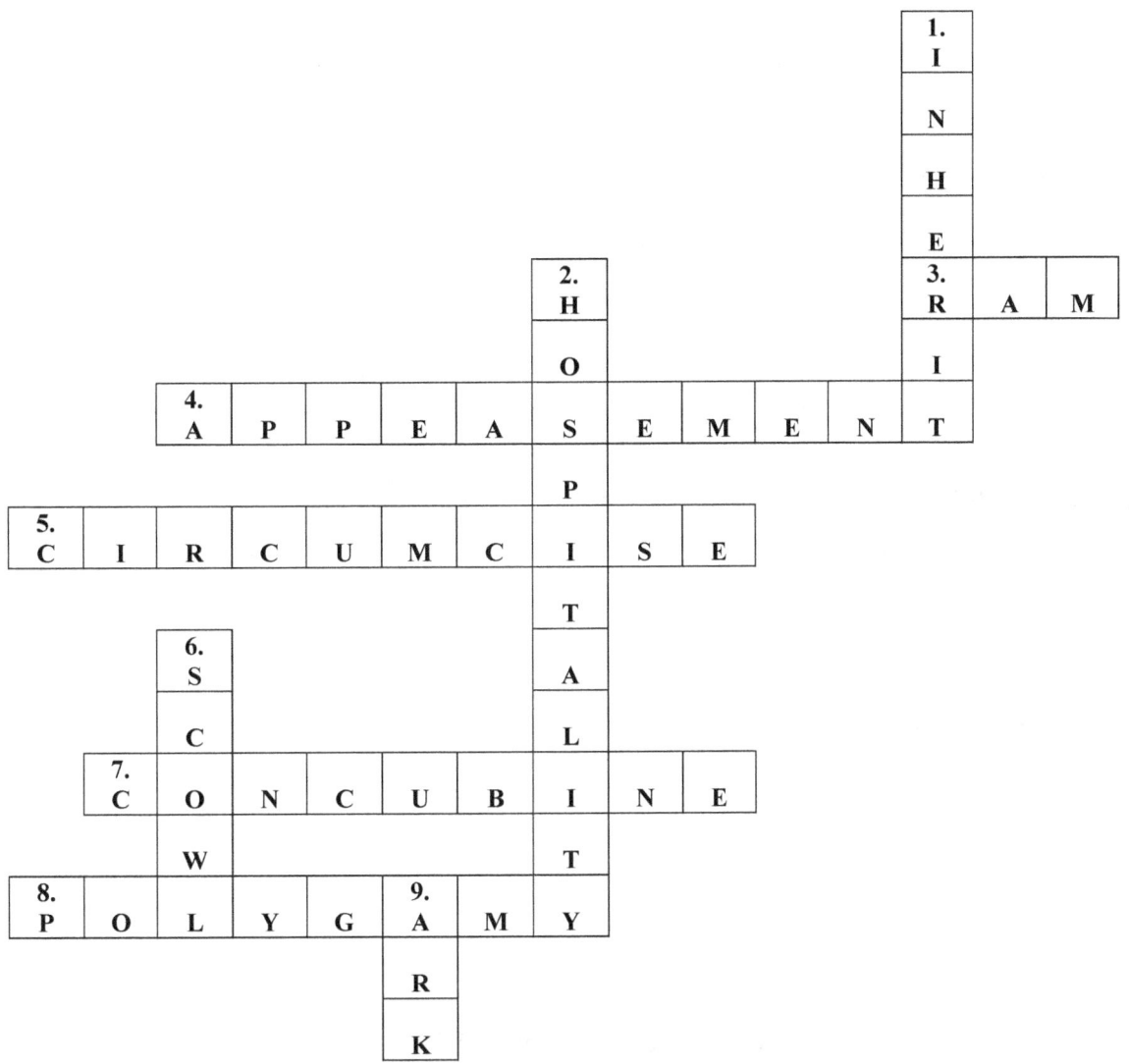

ACROSS:
3. A male sheep
4. The act of pacifying or buying off
5. Cut off the foreskin of a penis
7. A woman who is not a wife, but holds a recognized position in the household
8. Having more than one wife or husband at a time

DOWN:
1. Receive as an heir
2. A friendly and generous reception
6. An angry, wrinkled facial expression
9. A huge boat

Name: _____   Date: _____

Chapters 12-14: Abraham – Isaac Quiz

1. Who was Abram's wife?
   _____

2. Why did Abram and Lot split up?
   _____

3. Where did they go?
   a. Lot went to _____
   b. Abram stayed in _____

4. What was the custom for making family decisions then?
   _____

5. What did God promise Abram?
   _____

6. Who arranged for Hagar to have Abram's child? Why?
   _____
   _____

7. What did the angel promise Hagar?
   _____

8. What was the name of Abram and Hagar's son? _____

(Over)

9. What was the physical sign of God's covenant with Abraham?

   _____

10. What was the name of Sarah's son? _____

11. What did Sarah ask Abraham to do with Hagar and her son? Why?

    _____
    _____

12. How did Abraham feel? Why?

    _____

13. What did God command Abraham to do with his son, Isaac?

    _____
    _____

14. Why did God tell Abraham that?

    _____

15. Who was Isaac's wife?

    _____

I have neither given nor received any assistance on this quiz.

_____

Signature   Date

Name: _____   Date: _____

Chapters 12–14: Abraham – Isaac Quiz

1. Who was Abram's wife?

   Sarai

2. Why did Abram and Lot split up?

   There was not enough pasture land for their two flocks.

3. Where did they go?

   a. Lot went to **the Jordan Valley**

   b. Abram stayed in **the Central Mountain region of Canaan near Hebron.**

4. What was the custom for making family decisions then?

   It was the custom to defer to the elder in making family decisions.

5. What did God promise Abram?

   God promised Abram a son, many descendants.

6. Who arranged for Hagar to have Abram's child? Why?

   Sarai told Abram to try to have a child with her slave.

   They had lived ten years in Canaan and still had no children.

7. What did the angel promise Hagar?

   The angel promised Hagar many descendants.

8. What was the name of Abram and Hagar's son?

   Ishmael

(Over)

9. What was the physical sign of God's covenant with Abraham?

   Circumcision.

10. What was the name of Sarah's son?

    Isaac

11. What did Sarah ask Abraham to do with Hagar and her son? Why?

    She asked Abraham to send Hagar and Ishmael away so he could not inherit their wealth.

12. How did Abraham feel? Why?

    Abraham was quite troubled by her request because Ishmael was his first-born son.

13. What did God command Abraham to do with his son, Isaac?

    God commanded him to take Isaac to a mountain in Moriah and offer himn as a sacrifice to God.

14. Why did God tell Abraham that?

    God was testing whether Abraham would honor and obey him.

15. Who was Isaac's wife?

    Rebecca

I have neither given nor received any assistance on this quiz.

_____

Signature   Date

Name: _____   Date: _____

Chapter 15: Isaac

1. Where did Abraham send his servant to find a wife for his son, Isaac?

   _____
   _____

2. How did Rebecca show hospitality to the servant?

   _____

3. How did Laban show hospitality to the servant and his men?

   _____
   _____
   _____

4. Who had Isaac recently lost?

   _____

Name: _____   Date: _____

Chapter 15: Isaac

1. Where did Abraham send his servant to find a wife for his son, Isaac? (Genesis 24:4)

    The servant was to find a wife for Isaac among Abraham's relatives in Haran, Mesopotamia.

2. How did Rebecca show hospitality to the servant? (Gen 24:18-20)

    She not only gave him a drink but also filled the trough with water for his camels.

3. How did Laban show hospitality to the servant and his men? (Gen 24:31-33)

    Laban invited the men to come to their house. He unloaded the camels and gave them fodder to eat. He brought water for Abraham's servant and his men to wash their dusty feet. And then he brought them food as was customary in ancient times.

4. Who had Isaac recently lost? (Gen 24:67)

    His mother

Chapter 16: Isaac & Jacob

Student Activity: Group discussion on inheritances – then & now

1. Solicit student feelings about the favored position of the oldest male. How do you feel about the custom of the inheritance/birthright favoring to the oldest male?
    - They did not have courts to resolve family squabbles then. The inheritance custom was simple and clear.
    - Perhaps some parents made arrangements before their deaths to care for other children.
    - Perhaps the oldest son took care of his siblings.

Name: _____   Date: _____

Chapter 16: Isaac & Jacob

1. Who was Isaac's wife? _____

2. Which of the twin sons did Rebecca give birth to first? _____

3. Describe what Esau and Jacob were like.
   _____
   _____

4. Which son do you think each parent favored?
   _____

5. What did Esau give Jacob in exchange for some lentil soup (also known as bean soup)?
   _____

6. Who did Isaac ask to hunt and prepare food for him, so Isaac could bless him before he died? _____

7. Who actually prepared the food? Who brought it to Isaac?
   _____   _____

8. How did Jacob disguise himself as Esau?
   _____
   _____

(Over)

9. Who received Isaac's blessing? _____

10. When Esau brought food to Isaac what happened?
    _____

11. Why was Esau furious?
    _____

12. What did Rebecca do?
    _____

13. What did Esau do that upset his parents?
    _____

Name: _____   Date: _____

Chapter 16: Isaac & Jacob

1. Who was Isaac's wife? (Gen 24:51) **Rebecca**

2. Which of the twin sons did Rebecca give birth to first? (Gen 25:25-26) **Esau**

3. Describe what Esau and Jacob were like. (Gen 25:27)
   Esau was an outdoorsman and enjoyed hunting with his father. Jacob was quiet and preferred to stay at home. Most likely he was a shepherd.

4. Which son do you think each parent favored? (Gen 25:28)
   Isaac – Esau; Rebecca – Jacob

5. What did Esau give Jacob in exchange for some lentil soup (also known as bean soup)? (Gen 25:29-34) **His birthright (inheritance)**

6. Who did Isaac ask to hunt and prepare food for him, so Isaac could bless him before he died? (Gen 27:1-4) **Esau**

7. Who actually prepared the food? Who brought it to Isaac? (Gen 27:6-10)
   Rebecca. Jacob.

8. How did Jacob disguise himself as Esau? (Gen 27:15-16)
   He wore Esau's best clothes and put goat skins on his smooth arms.

(Over)

9. Who received Isaac's blessing? (Gen 27:25-29) **Jacob**

10. When Esau brought food to Isaac what happened? (Gen 27:30-33)
    Isaac trembled. He said he had been deceived by Jacob.

11. Why was Esau furious? (Gen 27: 41)
    Jacob had stolen the father's blessing intended for Esau.

12. What did Rebecca do? (Gen 27:43-45)
    She sent Jacob to stay with her brother, Laban, in Haran until Esau's anger cooled down.

13. What did Esau do that upset his parents? (Gen 27:46)
    Esau had previously married two Canaanite women, to his parents' dismay.

Chapter 17: Jacob

Supplemental Student Activity

1. Have students debate either in the round or as teams whether two wrongs made a right. Jacob created bitter feelings getting his brother's birthright and his father's blessing. Then Jacob was tricked into marrying Leah and working another seven years in order to marry his true love, Rachel. Does Jacob tricking his brother justify Laban tricking Jacob?

Closing Thought

Our decisions may come from insights, conversations, or just the courage to do what is right.

Name: _____   Date: _____

Chapter 17: Jacob

1. What did Jacob see in his dream while traveling to Mesopotamia?
   _____

2. What did Jacob promise to give to God if God blessed him on his journey?
   _____

3. Whom did Jacob fall in love with? _____

4. Explain the marriage custom of that time for the groom.
   _____
   _____

5. How was Jacob tricked? What did Jacob have to do?
   _____
   _____

6. How many sons did Jacob have? Who did the sons become?
   _____

7. When Jacob returned to his homeland, how did he feel? What did he do about it?
   _____
   _____

8. How did wrestling with an angel affect Jacob physically?
   _____

9. What does the angel change Jacob's name to? _____

Name: _____   Date: _____

Chapter 17: Jacob

1. What did Jacob see in his dream while traveling to Mesopotamia? (Gen 28:12)
   He dreamt of a stairway (or ladder) from earth to heaven with angels moving up and down.

2. What did Jacob promise to give to God if God blessed him on his journey? (Gen 28:22)
   He would give God a tenth (tithe) of everything he received if he, Jacob, had a safe journey.

3. Who did Jacob fall in love with? (Gen 29:10-12) **Rachel**

4. Explain the marriage custom of that time for the groom. (Gen 29:18)
   It was customary for the groom to offer the bride's parents a substantial gift to obtain their permission to marry their daughter.

5. How was Jacob tricked? What did Jacob have to do? (Gen 29:26-27)
   Laban substituted his heavily veiled, oldest daughter, Leah, for Rachel. Jacob had to work another seven years in order to marry his true love, Rachel.

6. How many sons did Jacob have? Who did the sons become? (Gen 35:22-26)
   Twelve sons. They become the heads of the twelve tribes of Israel.

7. When Jacob returned to his homeland, how did he feel? What did he do about it? (Gen 32:13-21)
   He worried about how he had treated Esau in trading for his birthright and stealing his father's blessing and how Esau had wanted to kill him in revenge for tricking him. He sent messengers ahead to tell Esau that he was coming as his obedient servant. Jacob chose a gift from his livestock to send to Esau.

8. How did wrestling with a man affect Jacob physically? (Gen 32:25)
   The man (angel) threw Jacob's hip out of joint. Jacob walked with a limp.

9. What does the angel change Jacob's name to? (Gen 32:28) **Israel**

Crossword Puzzle Chapters 15-17

ACROSS:

2. Solemn promise
3. An edible legume that is a dietary staple
5. To give one-tenth, usually in support of a church

DOWN:

1. A coarse, dry food, such as corn stalks, for livestock
4. A long, shallow, open box-like container to feed or water animals
6. A statue worshipped as a representation of a god

Crossword Puzzle Chapters 15-17

		1. F			
2. V	O	W			
		D			
		D			
3. L	E	N	4. T	I	L
		R	R		
			O		
			U		
			G		
5. T	6. I	T	H	E	
	D				
	O				
	L				

ACROSS:
2. Solemn promise
3. An edible legume that is a dietary staple
5. To give one-tenth, usually in support of a church

DOWN:
1. A coarse, dry food, such as corn stalks, for livestock
4. A long, shallow, open box-like container to feed or water animals
6. A statue worshipped as a representation of a god

Name: _____   Date: _____

Chapters 15-17: Isaac & Jacob Quiz

1. What did Esau give Jacob in exchange for some lentil soup?
   a. pastureland
   b. his first-born son
   c. his rights as the first-born son
   d. seven lambs

2. Whom did Isaac ask to prepare food for him as he drew near to death?
   a. Rebecca
   b. Esau
   c. Jacob
   d. Rachel

3. How did Jacob commit deception to obtain Isaac's blessing?
   a. promised Esau many descendants
   b. disguised himself as Esau
   c. promised Esau plentiful harvests
   d. gave Esau food

4. Where did Isaac send Jacob to find a wife for himself?
   a. Egypt
   b. Jerusalem
   c. Jordan Valley
   d. Haran

5. What did Jacob see in his dream while traveling?
   a. a huge flock
   b. a tower to heaven
   c. a stairway
   d. a well

6. How was Jacob deceived by Laban?
   a. Laban tricked him into exploring for him
   b. Laban promised him wealth
   c. Laban sold him dry wells
   d. Laban tricked him into marrying his older daughter, Leah.

7. On his way home Jacob had another dream. It was about:
   a. deceiving Abimelech
   b. wrestling with a man
   c. a famine
   d. saving Esau

(Over)

8. What was the new name that the angel gave to Jacob?
   - a. Yahweh
   - b. Abraham
   - c. Israel
   - d. Canaan

9. lentil
   - a. flat bean
   - b. carrot
   - c. tomato
   - d. corn

10. vow
    - a. worship
    - b. voice
    - c. a solemn promise
    - d. a male sheep

11. tithe
    - a. title
    - b. one-tenth
    - c. tip
    - d. tin

12. idol
    - a. embark
    - b. tribal leader
    - c. embargo
    - d. a statue worshipped as a god

I have neither given nor received any assistance on this quiz.

_____

Signature   Date

Name: _____   Date: _____

Chapters 15-17: Isaac & Jacob Quiz

1. What did Esau give Jacob in exchange for some lentil soup?
    a. pastureland
    c. his rights as the first-born son
    b. his first-born son
    d. seven lambs

2. Whom did Isaac ask to prepare food for him as he drew near to death?
    a. Rebecca
    c. Jacob
    b. Esau
    d. Rachel

3. How did Jacob commit deception to obtain Isaac's blessing?
    a. promised Esau many descendants
    b. disguised himself as Esau
    c. promised Esau plentiful harvests
    d. gave Esau food

4. Where did Isaac send Jacob to find a wife for himself?
    a. Egypt
    c. Jordan Valley
    b. Jerusalem
    d. Haran

5. What did Jacob see in his dream while traveling?
    a. a huge flock
    c. a stairway
    b. a tower to heaven
    d. a well

6. How was Jacob deceived by Laban?
    a. Laban tricked him into exploring for him
    b. Laban promised him wealth
    c. Laban sold him dry wells
    d. Laban tricked him into marrying his older daughter, Leah.

7. On his way home Jacob had another dream. It was about:
    a. deceiving Abimelech
    c. a famine
    b. wrestling with a man
    d. saving Esau

(Over)

8. What was the new name that the man gave to Jacob?
   - a. Yahweh
   - **c. Israel**
   - b. Abraham
   - d. Canaan

9. lentil
   - a. **flat bean**
   - c. tomato
   - b. carrot
   - d. corn

10. vow
    - a. worship
    - **c. a solemn promise**
    - b. voice
    - d. a male sheep

11. tithe
    - a. title
    - c. tip
    - b. **one-tenth**
    - d. tin

12. idol
    - a. embark
    - c. embargo
    - b. tribal leader
    - **d. a statue worshipped as a god**

I have neither given nor received any assistance on this quiz.

_____

Signature   Date

Chapter 18: Joseph & His Brothers

Supplemental Student Activities

1. Draw a family tree of the patriarchs of Israel (i.e., Abraham, Isaac, Jacob, and Joseph). Include their wives and their sons.

2. Estimate the distance from Canaan to Goshen. You are approximating the distance Joseph walked in slavery to Egypt. (Estimate: 210 miles)

3. Bible Search- Genesis 37: Cite four reasons with chapter & verse why Joseph's brothers hated him.
    a. 37:2. He brought bad reports to his father about what his brothers were doing.
    b. 37:3. Jacob loved Joseph more because he was the first-born son of his true love, Rachel.
    c. 37:3. Jacob made a long robe with full sleeves for Joseph.
    d. 37:6-8. Joseph said, "Listen to the dream I had. We were all in the field tying up sheaves of wheat, when my sheaf got up and stood up straight. Yours formed a circle around mine and bowed down to it." "Do you think you are going to be a king and rule over us?" his brothers asked. So, they hated him even more…

Role Play or Discussion Activity: (Adapted from Cain's Children, A Course of Study, by Caroline Pineo. Philadelphia: Friends General Conference, 1970. Paraphrased.)

There are two sons, Kevin and Sean, living with their mother.

You are Kevin. Kevin is the same age as you. You have a younger brother, Sean. Your mother comes home from work one day and says a co-worker has invited her to go to an amusement park (e.g., Kings Dominion, etc.) next weekend with her and her son. However, your Mom can only bring one son. There isn't room in the car for anyone else. And her co-worker has only two special discount tickets. So, your Mom can take only one of you, either Kevin or Sean. You both want to go. She finally decides to take Sean.

How did you feel?

You are Sean. How did you feel?

How do you think the mother felt about having to choose between her two sons?

Name: _____   Date: _____

Chapter 18: Joseph & His Brothers

1. How many sons did Jacob have? _____

2. What garment did Joseph's father give him?
   _____

3. How did Joseph's brothers interpret Joseph's dream?
   _____

4. What did Joseph's father understand the second dream to mean?
   _____

5. Describe 3 reasons Joseph's brothers hated him.
   _____
   _____
   _____

6. Which brother intervened to save Joseph's life? _____

7. Who proposed that the brothers sell Joseph to the Ishmaelites? _____

8. What did the brothers decide to tell their father about Jacob?
   _____
   _____

9. Who purchased Joseph in Egypt?
   _____

Name: _____   Date: _____

Chapter 18: Joseph & His Brothers

1. How many sons did Jacob have? (Gen 35:22) **12**

2. What garment did Joseph's father give him? (Gen 37:3)
   A beautiful, fine, long robe with sleeves when most shepherds wore coarse, short sleeve tunics.

3. How did Joseph's brothers interpret Joseph's dream? (Gen 37:6-8)
   They believed that Joseph thought he would be a king and rule over them.

4. What did Joseph's father understand the second dream to mean? (Gen 37:9-10)
   That he, his wife, and Joseph's brothers were going to bow down before Joseph.

5. Describe 3 reasons Joseph's brothers hated him (Gen 37:3-10)
   He loved Joseph more because he was the first-born son of his true love, Rachel.
   His father gave him a beautiful, fine, long robe with sleeves
   He brought bad reports to his father about what his brothers were doing.
   His dreams implied that he would rule over them.

6. Which brother intervened to save Joseph's life? (Gen 37:21-22) **Reuben**

7. Who proposed that the brothers sell Joseph to the Ishmaelites? (Gen 37:26-27) **Judah**

8. What did the brothers decide to tell their father about Jacob? (Gen 37:31-33)
   They dipped Joseph's robe in goat's blood and told their father that a wild animal killed Joseph.

9. Who purchased Joseph in Egypt? (Gen 37: 36) **Potiphar, the captain of the pharaoh's palace guard**

Name: _____   Date: _____

Chapter 19: Joseph & the Wife of the Captain of the Palace Guard

1. How did Joseph fare in Potiphar's house?

   _____
   _____
   _____

2. How did Joseph respond when his master's wife tempted him?

   _____
   _____
   _____

3. Why was the jailer pleased with Joseph?

   _____
   _____
   _____

4. What do you think the moral lesson is that the author is conveying in this story?

   _____
   _____
   _____

Name: _____   Date: _____

Chapter 19: Joseph & the Wife of the Captain of the Palace Guard

1. How did Joseph fare in Potiphar's house? (Gen 39:2-6)

   Joseph worked hard and was successful at the tasks assigned. As a result, Potiphar make Joseph his personal servant and put him in charge of his house and everything he owned.

2. How did Joseph respond when his master's wife tempted him? (Gen 39:8-10)

   He refused and explained how his master, her husband, had trusted him and put him in charge of everything. "How could I do such an immoral thing and sin against God?"

3. Why was the jailer pleased with Joseph? (Gen 39:23)

   The jailer noticed his good work and was pleased. (in other words, Joseph made the most of the situation. He did what was assigned as well as he could and without an attitude.)

4. What do you think the moral lesson is that the author is conveying in this story?

   Making the best of a bad situation

   Dependability

   Integrity

Name: _____   Date: _____

Chapter 20: Joseph Interprets Dreams & Becomes Governor of Egypt

1. Who did the king imprison with Joseph?
   _____

2. Who interpreted the dreams of those imprisoned by the king? _____

3. What did the king do to the chief wine steward and the chief baker?
   _____
   _____

4. What did Joseph interpret the king's dreams to mean?
   _____
   _____

5. Who did the king place in charge of preparations for the time of famine?
   _____

6. What did Joseph do during the seven years of plenty?
   _____

7. What did Joseph do when the people faced famine?
   _____
   _____

Name: _____   Date: _____

Chapter 20: Joseph Interprets Dreams & Becomes Governor of Egypt

1. Who did king imprison with Joseph? (Gen 40:1-3)

   He imprisoned the chief wine steward and the chief baker.

2. Who interpreted the dreams of those imprisoned by the king? (Gen 40:6-19)

   Joseph did.

3. What did the king do to the chief wine steward and the chief baker? (Gen 40:21-22)

   He restored the chief wine steward to his position and executed the chief baker.

4. What did Joseph interpret the king's dreams to mean? (Gen 41:25-36)

   He said that Egypt would experience seven years of good livestock and grain followed by seven years of severe famine.

5. Who did the king place in charge of preparations for the time of famine? (Gen 41:37-46)

   Joseph

6. What did Joseph do during the seven years of plenty? (Gen 41:34; Gen 41:47-49)

   He had one-fifth of the grain warehoused.

7. What did Joseph do when the people faced famine? (Gen 41:55-57)

   He opened all the storehouses and sold the grain to the Egyptians and to people from other countries.

Chapter 21: Joseph's Brothers Go to Egypt & Return There with Benjamin

Supplemental Student Activities

1. Ask your students what Joseph could have done when his brothers arrived. Possible answers:

    a. not give them food and make them go back home;

    b. identify himself and tell them of the horrible way they treated him years before;

    c. identify himself and forgive them for what they did; or

    d. identify himself and put them in jail.

2. Have students divide into teams to defend one point. After the initial round of discussion, ask which point enables the family to reconcile and unite again.

Name: _____ Date: _____

Chapter 21: Joseph's Brothers Go to Egypt & Return There with Benjamin

1. Why did Jacob send his sons to Egypt?

   _____

2. Why did Jacob not allow Benjamin to go to Egypt?

   _____

3. What did Joseph give as the reason for his brothers' coming into the land of Egypt?

   _____

4. Who did Joseph keep as a hostage when he let the brothers return to Canaan with grain?

   _____

5. How were the brothers to obtain the release of Simeon?

   _____

6. How did Reuben's rebuke of the other brothers for their mistreatment of Joseph affect Joseph?

   _____

7. What did the brothers discover in the tops of their bags of grain?

   _____

(Over)

8. How did Jacob respond to the demand that the brothers take Benjamin to Egypt?

9. Why did Jacob send his sons to Egypt a second time?

10. How did Judah get his father to agree to let the brothers take Benjamin with them?

11. Why did the brothers think they were brought to Joseph's house?

12. What did Joseph do when he saw Benjamin?

In your opinion why can forgiveness be better in the long run than getting even?

Name: _____   Date: _____

Chapter 21: Joseph's Brothers Go to Egypt & Return There with Benjamin

1. Why did Jacob send his sons to Egypt? (Gen 42:2)
   Because they were having a famine and because Egypt had grain, Jacob sent his sons there.

2. Why did Jacob not allow Benjamin to go to Egypt? (Gen 42:4)
   Jacob was afraid something might happen to him, his only surviving son of his true love, Rachel.

3. What did Joseph give as the reason for his brothers' coming into the land of Egypt? (Gen 42:9, 14)
   He accused them of being spies.

4. Who did Joseph keep as a hostage when he let the brothers return to Canaan with grain? (Gen 42: 24)
   He kept Simeon.

5. How were the brothers to obtain the release of Simeon? (Gen 42:20)
   They were to obtain his release by returning with their youngest brother, Benjamin.

6. How did Reuben's rebuke of the other brothers for their mistreatment of Joseph affect Joseph? (Gen 42:24) **He left them for a minute and cried.**

7. What did the brothers discover in the tops of their bags of grain? (Gen 42:27)
   They found their money had been returned.

(Over)

8. How did Jacob respond to the demand that the brothers take Benjamin to Egypt? (Gen 42:36)

    He refused to let Benjamin go. "Do you want me to lose all my children." (Gen 42:36) (GNT)

9. Why did Jacob send his sons to Egypt a second time? (Gen 43:1-2)

    They returned because they had eaten all the grain they brought from Egypt.

10. How did Judah get his father to agree to let the brothers take Benjamin with them? (Gen 43:4-10)

    Judah pledged his own life to guarantee Benjamin's safety.

11. Why did the brothers think they were brought to Joseph's house? (Gen 43:18)

    They were worried about being attacked and enslaved.

12. What did Joseph do when he saw Benjamin? (Gen 43:29-30)

    He left the room and cried.

In your opinion why can forgiveness be better in the long run than getting even?

_____
_____
_____
_____

Chapter 22: The Missing Cup and Joseph Identifies Himself

Supplemental Student Activity

1. Open discussion: Share examples of someone forgiving another. Describe the situation, the forgiveness, and how the forgiven person felt. Also, how the person forgiving felt.

Name: _____   Date: _____

Chapter 22: The Missing Cup and Joseph Identifies Himself

1. What did Joseph order his steward to place in Benjamin's sack along with the food and the money?
   _____

2. How did the brothers react when Joseph's steward found the cup in Benjamin's sack?
   _____

3. Who did Joseph say would be his slave?
   _____

4. What did Judah offer to do to free Benjamin?
   _____

5. How did Joseph explain his brothers' deed of selling him into slavery?
   _____

6. What did Joseph tell his brothers to do?
   _____

7. What was the king's reaction to the news that Joseph's brothers had come to Egypt?
   _____

Name: _____   Date: _____

Chapter 22: The Missing Cup and Joseph Identifies Himself

1. What did Joseph order his steward to place in Benjamin's sack along with the food and the money? (Gen 44:2)

   He had his own special, silver cup placed in the sack.

2. How did the brothers react when Joseph's steward found the cup in Benjamin's sack? (Gen 44:13)

   They tore their garments in sorrow and returned to Joseph's house.

3. Who did Joseph say would be his slave? (Gen 44:17)

   He demanded the one who had his cup.

4. What did Judah offer to do to free Benjamin? (Gen 44:33-34)

   He said that he would stay as Joseph's slave in place of Benjamin.

5. How did Joseph explain his brothers' deed of selling him into slavery? (Gen 45:5)

   Joseph credited God for sending him ahead of them to Egypt to save people's lives.

6. What did Joseph tell his brothers to do? (Gen 45:9-10)

   He told them to tell their father that he is alive and to return to Egypt with the whole family to live in the Goshen area.

7. What was the king's reaction to the news that Joseph's brothers had come to Egypt? (Gen 45:16-20)

   The king also wanted Joseph's extended family to settle in Egypt.

Name: _____   Date: _____

Chapter 23: Jacob's Family Moves to Egypt & Famine Strikes Harder

1. How many direct descendants of Jacob plus their wives moved to Egypt?

   _____

2. Why did Joseph tell his father and brothers to tell the king that they were shepherds?

   _____

   _____

3. When the Egyptians had no more money to buy grain, what did Joseph first buy from them in place of money?

   _____

4. After they sold their land to Joseph, what did the Egyptians next do in exchange for grain?

   _____

Name: _____   Date: _____

Chapter 23: Jacob's Family Moves to Egypt & Famine Strikes Harder

1. How many direct descendants of Jacob plus their wives moved to Egypt? (Gen 46:26-27)

   Sixty-six direct descendants plus their wives moved to Egypt.

2. Why did Joseph tell his father and brothers to tell the king that they were shepherds? (Gen 46:33-34)

   The Egyptians will have nothing to do with shepherds. Egyptians were farmers who always worried about herds eating their crops.

3. When the Egyptians had no more money to buy grain, what did Joseph first buy from them in place of money? (Gen 47:15-17)

   He bought their livestock.

4. After they sold their land to Joseph, what did the Egyptians next do in exchange for grain? (Gen 47:18-19)

   They offered themselves as his slaves.

Chapter 24: Jacob's Last Request, Blessing, and Death

Supplemental Discussion Activities

1. Joseph made the lives of his fellow citizens better during the famine. He took the lead in reconciling with his brothers and in bringing his family together again. Consider how you have made life better for others. How have you helped your family?

2. Think how your own negative experiences have turned out well.

3. What causes problems among family members? What can minimize them?

Supplemental Student Activities

1. Write a newspaper on Joseph stories. Include a weather report & editorial. Drawing(s).

2. Discuss how Joseph has grown in this story.

3. Discuss how Joseph's brothers have grown in this story.

Name: _____   Date: _____

Chapter 24: Jacob's Last Request, Blessing, and Death

1. Who did Joseph bring with him when he heard that his father was ill?
   _____

2. Which of Joseph's two sons received the greater blessing from Jacob – the older or younger son?
   _____

3. What did Joseph have done to his father's body in Egypt?
   _____

4. Where did Jacob request that his sons bury him?
   _____

5. What did Joseph's brothers fear from Joseph after the death of their father?
   _____

6. How did Joseph explain his brothers' mistreatment of him?
   _____
   _____
   _____

(Over)

In your opinion how has Joseph grown over the whole story? Support your points with examples.

_____
_____
_____
_____
_____

In your opinion how have Joseph's brothers grown over the whole story? Support your points with examples.

_____
_____
_____
_____
_____

Name: _____   Date: _____

Chapter 24: Jacob's Last Request, Blessing, and Death

1. Who did Joseph bring with him when he heard that his father was ill? (Gen 48:1-2)

   He took his sons, Manasseh and Ephraim, to see Jacob.

2. Which of Joseph's two sons received the greater blessing from Jacob – the older or younger son? (Gen 48:13-20)

   Ephraim did. He was the younger son.

3. What did Joseph have done to his father's body in Egypt? (Gen 50:2-3)

   He had the body embalmed.

4. Where did Jacob request that his sons bury him? (Gen 49:29-32)

   He requested that Joseph bury him in Canaan.

5. What did Joseph's brothers fear from Joseph after the death of their father? (Gen 50:15)

   They feared his retribution for their earlier mistreatment of him.

6. How did Joseph explain his brothers' mistreatment of him? (Gen 50:19-20)

   Joseph told them not to be afraid, that he will not put himself in the place of God and judge them, and that God had turned their evil deed into good and saved many people.

   (Over)

In your opinion how has Joseph grown over the whole story? Support your points with examples.

___

In your opinion how have Joseph's brothers grown over the whole story? Support your points with examples.

___

Crossword Puzzle Chapters 18-24

ACROSS:
3. To eat greedily
5. Treat a corpse with preservatives to prevent decay
6. A group of travelers
9. Using omens or magic powers to tell the future
11. A dry well; a tank or large pottery jar for storing water

DOWN:
1. A bundle of stalks
2. An Egyptian king
4. Revenge; retaliation
7. Promise to pay if the product or service is not done
8. A principle
10. Dry or shrivel in the heat

Crossword Puzzle Chapters 18-24

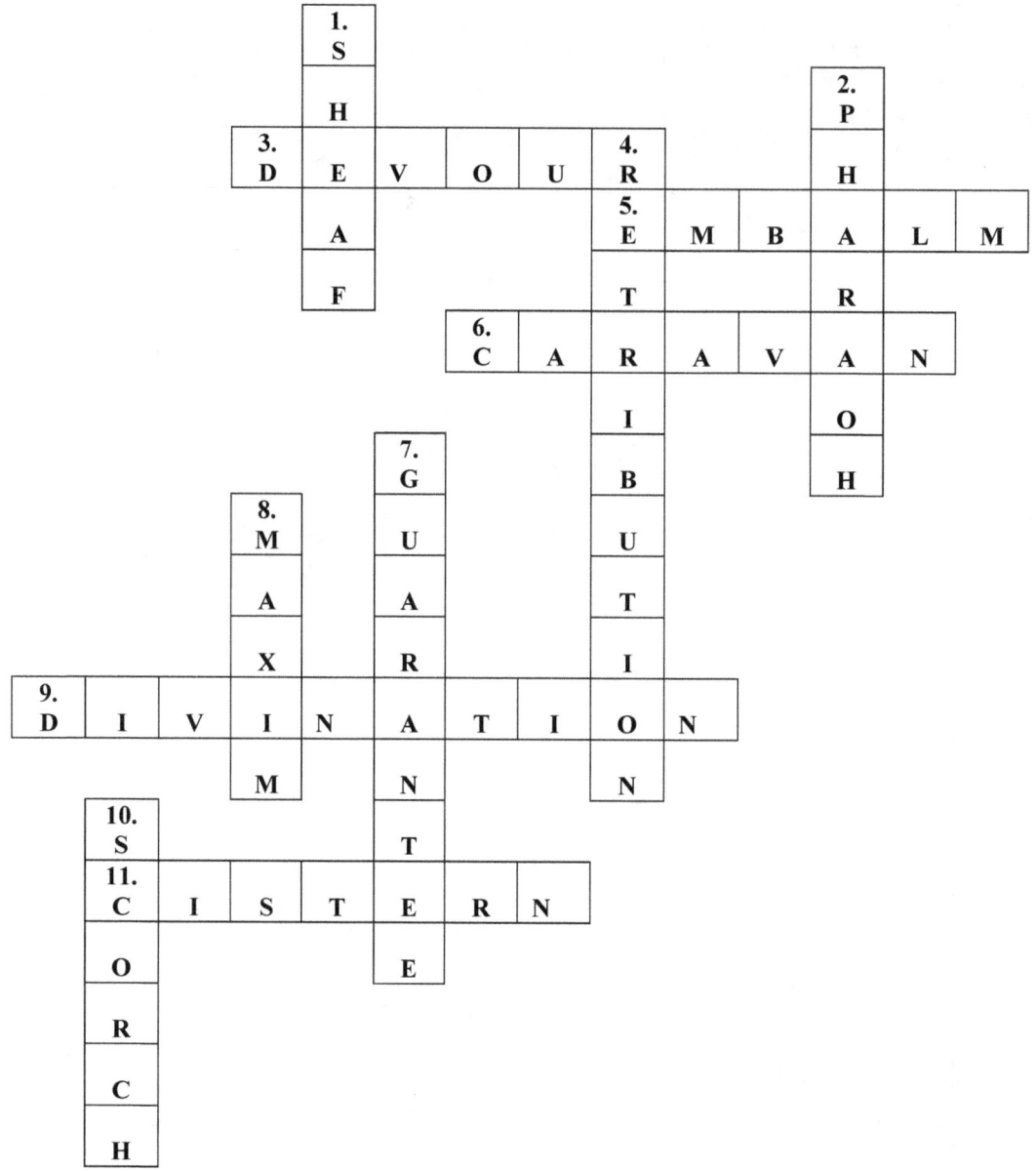

ACROSS:
3. To eat greedily
5. Treat a corpse with preservatives to prevent decay
6. A group of travelers
9. Using omens or magic powers to tell the future
11. A dry well; a tank or large pottery jar for storing water

DOWN:
1. A bundle of stalks
2. An Egyptian king
4. Revenge; retaliation
7. Promise to pay if the product or service is not done
8. A principle
10. Dry or shrivel in the heat

Name: _____   Date _____

Chapters 18-24: Joseph Quiz

Read each question carefully. Circle the letter that best answers the question.

1. Why did Joseph's brothers hate him?
    a. He was his mother's favorite.
    b. He was a very productive shepherd.
    c. He was a very successful farmer.
    d. He was his father's favorite son.

2. How did Joseph fare as a slave in Potiphar's house?
    a. He was successful. Potiphar turned everything over to Joseph.
    b. He was successful. Potiphar worked him hard.
    c. He was unsuccessful. Potiphar despised him.
    d. He was unsuccessful. Potiphar sold him.

3. Why was Joseph imprisoned?
    a. Potiphar was upset with his work.
    b. The king was furious with Joseph for his remarks to Potiphar's wife.
    c. Joseph owed taxes to the king.
    d. Potiphar's wife betrayed him after he refused her advances.

4. While in prison, Joseph interpreted the dreams of a chief wine steward and a chief baker as follows.
    a. The king will restore the wine steward to his position and execute the chief baker.
    b. The king will restore Joseph to his position.
    c. The king will threaten to kill the wine steward, the baker, and Joseph.
    d. The king will release the wine steward, the baker, and Joseph from prison.

5. How did Joseph interpret the king's dream?
    a. The king will have many descendants.
    b. Egypt will experience seven years of plenty, followed by seven years of drought.
    c. Egypt will become an empire and rule other nations.
    d. The king will be killed in battle.

(Over)

6. How did Joseph come to be appointed the governor of Egypt?
   a. The king liked Joseph's work as his personal servant.
   b. The king appreciated Joseph's integrity in refusing Potiphar's wife's advances.
   c. The king was impressed with Joseph's ancestors.
   d. The king was impressed with Joseph's advice on how to prepare for a famine.

7. How did Reuben's rebuke of his brothers for their mistreatment of Joseph affect Joseph?
   a. Joseph rejoiced.   c. Joseph left the room and cried.
   b. Joseph threw all of them in prison.   d. Joseph praised Reuben.

8. Why did Jacob send his sons to Egypt a second time?
   a. They ate all the grain they brought from Egypt.   c. They needed pasture land.
   b. They were seeking a better place to worship.   d. They had an argument.

9. Who must Joseph's brothers bring to Egypt on their return trip?
   a. Rueben   c. Simeon
   b. Jacob   d. Benjamin

10. What did Joseph order his steward to place in Benjamin's bag along with grain and money?
    a. Joseph's silver cup   c. A gem
    b. A sword   d. A testament

11. Why did Joseph tell his father and brothers to tell the king that they were shepherds?
    a. So they did not compete with the farmers and cause resentment.
    b. The Egyptians needed sheep.
    c. Shepherds were detested by the Egyptians. They would be able to settle away from the Egyptians.
    d. The Egyptians loved shepherds.

12. When the Egyptians had no money to buy grain, what did Joseph first take from them in place of money?
    a. their wives   c. their livestock
    b. their concubines   d. their first-born sons

13. Which of Joseph's sons received the greater blessing from Jacob?
    a. the older son, Manasseh   b. the younger son, Ephraim

(Over)

115

14. Sheaf means:
    a. a bundle of stalks
    b. a long garment
    c. a sprout
    d. a group of travelers

15. Caravan means:
    a. a bundle of stalks
    b. a long garment
    c. a sprout
    d. a group of travelers

I have neither given nor received any assistance on this quiz.

_____

Signature					Date

Name: _____   Date _____

Chapters 18-24: Joseph Quiz

Read each question carefully. Circle the letter that best answers the question.

1. Why did Joseph's brothers hate him?
   a. He was his mother's favorite.
   b. He was a very productive shepherd.
   c. He was a very successful farmer.
   d. He was his father's favorite son.

2. How did Joseph fare as a slave in Potiphar's house?
   a. He was successful. Potiphar turned everything over to Joseph.
   b. He was successful. Potiphar worked him hard.
   c. He was unsuccessful. Potiphar despised him.
   d. He was unsuccessful. Potiphar sold him.

3. Why was Joseph imprisoned?
   a. Potiphar was upset with his work.
   b. The king was furious with Joseph for his remarks to Potiphar's wife.
   c. Joseph owed taxes to the king.
   d. Potiphar's wife betrayed him after he refused her advances.

4. While in prison, Joseph interpreted the dreams of a chief wine steward and a chief baker as follows.
   a. The king will restore the wine steward to his position and execute the chief baker.
   b. The king will restore Joseph to his position.
   c. The king will threaten to kill the wine steward, the baker, and Joseph.
   d. The king will release the wine steward, the baker, and Joseph from prison.

5. How did Joseph interpret the king's dream?
   a. The king will have many descendants.
   b. Egypt will experience seven years of plenty, followed by seven years of drought.
   c. Egypt will become an empire and rule other nations.
   d. The king will be killed in battle.

(Over)

6. How did Joseph come to be appointed the governor of Egypt?
   a. The king liked Joseph's work as his personal servant.
   b. The king appreciated Joseph's integrity in refusing Potiphar's wife's advances.
   c. The king was impressed with Joseph's ancestors.
   d. **The king was impressed with Joseph's advice on how to prepare for a famine**.

7. How did Reuben's rebuke of his brothers for their mistreatment of Joseph affect Joseph?
   a. Joseph rejoiced.   **c. Joseph left the room and cried.**
   b. Joseph threw all of them in prison.   d. Joseph praised Reuben.

8. Why did Jacob send his sons to Egypt a second time?
   a. **They ate all the grain they brought from Egypt**.   c. They needed pasture land.
   b. They were seeking a better place to worship.   d. They had an argument.

9. Who must Joseph's brothers bring to Egypt on their return trip?
   a. Rueben
   b. Jacob
   c. Simeon
   d. **Benjamin**

10. What did Joseph order his steward to place in Benjamin's bag along with grain and money?
    a. **Joseph's silver cup**
    b. A sword
    c. A gem
    d. A testament

11. Why did Joseph tell his father and brothers to tell the king that they were shepherds?
    a. So they did not compete with the farmers and cause resentment.
    b. The Egyptians needed sheep.
    c. Shepherds were detested by the Egyptians. They would be able to settle away from the Egyptians.
    d. The Egyptians loved shepherds.

12. When the Egyptians had no money to buy grain, what did Joseph first take from them in place of money?
    a. their wives
    b. their concubines
    c. their livestock
    d. their first-born sons

13. Which of Joseph's sons received the greater blessing from Jacob?
    a. the older son, Manasseh
    b. **the younger, son, Ephraim**

(Over)

14. Sheaf means:
   a. **a bundle of stalks**
   b. a long garment
   c. a sprout
   d. a group of travelers

15. Caravan means:
   c. a bundle of stalks
   d. a long garment
   c. a sprout
   d. **a group of travelers**

I have neither given nor received any assistance on this quiz.

_____

Signature   Date

Chapter 25: Moses' Early Life

Supplemental Discussion Activities

1. In the first two chapters of Exodus, several women in two separate incidents (i.e., Shiphrah & Puah and Moses' sister and mother) demonstrate tremendous courage and nonviolent action in helping other people at the risk of their own safety. Describe both incidents. Why did they care? Who did they defy? (Ex 1:15- Ex 2:10)
    a. The King felt threatened by the numerous Israelites. Therefore, he ordered two midwives, Shiphrah and Puah, who helped Israeli women at childbirth, to kill their male babies. But the midwives were God-fearing and did not obey the king. When confronted by the king, they made up a story that the Israelite women give birth easily and their babies are born before the midwives get there. Shiphrah and Puah demonstrated great courage in defying the king through their nonviolent disobedience.
    b. The king then directs his people to take every newborn Hebrew boy and throw him into the Nile. Moses' mother placed Moses in a watertight basket and hid him in the reeds along the edge of the Nile. She had his sister keep a watch on him. However, the king's daughter came to the river to bathe, saw the basket in the tall reeds, opened it, and found a baby boy. Moses' sister then offered to find someone to nurse the baby. She returned with her mother. Moses' mother and sister demonstrated great courage in defying the King through their nonviolent intervention.

2. Discuss why the king wanted to kill the baby boys. Possible answers:
    a. Eliminate possible military threat: They might grow up to fight Egyptians.
    b. Reduce their population.
    c. Force women to marry Egyptians & become Egyptians.

3. Discuss the courage of the midwives: the non-violent action of the midwives
    a. What they risked vs. conscience.
    b. Doing the right thing is not easy or glamorous.

4. Discuss Moses' killing of the Egyptian foreman.
    a. Discuss pros/cons.
    b. Were Moses' actions honorable?

5. Assess impact of saving Moses on the world! By Miriam & her daughter and by the Egyptian princess, the king's daughter.
    a. Israel is eventually freed. Moses is the ancestor of Abraham who three major religions trace their roots to. The Moses Exodus story was an inspiration to enslaved African Americans.

Name: _____   Date: _____

Chapter 25: Moses' Early Life

1. List three factors that led to the enslavement of the Israelites in Egypt.

   _____
   _____
   _____

2. What did the king hope to accomplish by enslaving the Israelites?

   _____

3. What did the Egyptians force the people of Israel to do?

   _____
   _____

4. What did the king of Egypt tell the Egyptian midwives to do?

   _____

5. Why did the midwives, Shiphrah and Puah, disobey the king of Egypt? (Why did they care?)

   _____

6. What command did the king of Egypt give all his subjects?

   _____
   _____

(Over)

7. How did the Israelite woman attempt to save her son from death?

_____
_____
_____
_____
_____

8. Who nursed the baby boy for the king's daughter?

_____

9. Why did Moses kill the Egyptian?

_____

10. Where did Moses flee to? _____

11. Who did Moses marry? _____

Question: Did Moses do the right thing when he killed the Egyptian? First, describe what happened. Next, explain your position by giving reasons to support it.

_____
_____
_____
_____

Name: _____   Date: _____

Chapter 25: Moses' Early Life

1. List three factors that led to the enslavement of the Israelites in Egypt. (Ex 1:8-11)
   - **A new king, who did not know about Joseph, came to power.**
   - **The new king was concerned about how numerous the Israelites had become.**
   - **He worried that they might join their enemy if they were attacked.**

2. What did the king hope to accomplish by enslaving the Israelites? (Ex 1:10)
   He wanted to keep them from becoming even more numerous.

3. What did the Egyptians force the people of Israel to do? (Ex 1:11, 14)
   The Egyptians forced them to build the cities of Pithom and Rameses as supply centers and later as slaves constructing buildings and working in their fields under the blazing Egyptian sun.

4. What did the king of Egypt tell the Egyptian midwives to do? (Ex 1:16)
   The king told them to kill the baby Israelite boys and to let the baby girls live.

5. Why did the midwives, Shiphrah and Puah, disobey the king of Egypt? (Why did they care?) (Ex 1:17)
   The midwives were God-fearing.

6. What command did the king of Egypt give all his subjects? (Ex 1:22)
   He commanded them to throw every newborn Israelite boy into the Nile and to allow the girls to live.

(Over)

7. How did the Hebrew woman attempt to save her son from death? (Ex 2:3-4)

   She made a basket from the reeds that grew along the banks of the Nile and made it waterproof with a coating of tar. She hid her baby in the basket and wedged it among the reeds on the river bank. She assigned her older daughter, Miriam, to keep an eye on the basket from a distance.

8. Who nursed the baby boy for the king's daughter? (Ex 2:7-8)

   The baby's mother nursed him.

9. Why did Moses kill the Egyptian? (Ex 2:11-12)

   Moses killed the Egyptian overseer because he saw the Egyptian overseer kill an Israelite.

10. Where did Moses flee to? (Ex 2:15-16) **Midian in the Sinai Peninsula**

11. Who did Moses marry? (Ex 2:21) **Zipporah**

Question: Did Moses do the right thing when he killed the Egyptian? First, describe what happened. Next, explain your position by giving reasons to support it.

_____
_____
_____
_____

Name: _____   Date: _____

Chapter 26: The Ten Plagues

1. How did the king further oppress the people of Israel after Aaron and Moses visited him?
   _____

2. How did Moses confront God after the king further oppressed the people of Israel?
   _____
   _____

3. What was the nature of the first plague?
   _____

4. What was King's reaction to the first nine plagues?
   _____

5. What was the tenth and final plague?
   _____

6. What did the special Passover meal include?
   _____

7. Why did God instruct the Israelites to put some of the blood of the Passover lamb or goat on the doorposts and above the doors of the houses?
   _____
   _____

8. How did the King respond to the tenth plague?
   a. _____
   b. _____
   c. _____

Name: _____   Date: _____

Chapter 26: The Ten Plagues

1. How did the king further oppress the people of Israel after Aaron and Moses visited him? (Ex 5:6-9) **He commanded the Egyptian slave drivers to make them work harder.**

2. How did Moses confront God after the king further oppressed the people of Israel? (Ex 5:22-23) **Moses told God. "Why do you mistreat your people? Ever since I went to the king to speak for you, he has treated them cruelly. And you have done nothing to help them!"** (Ex 5:22-23) (GNT)

3. What was the nature of the first plague? (Ex 7:17-21) **The water of the Nile turned into blood.**

4. What was King's reaction to the first nine plagues? (Ex 7:22-23, etc.). **He refused to let the Israelites go.**

5. What was the tenth and final plague? (Ex 11:4-5) **The Angel of Death killed all the first-born Egyptian sons.**

6. What did the special Passover meal include? (Ex 12:5-9) **It included lamb (sheep) or goat meat, bitter herbs, and unleavened bread.**

7. Why did God instruct the Israelites to put some of the blood of the Passover lamb or goat on the doorposts and above the doors of the houses? (Ex 12:7,13) **The blood on the doorposts was a sign for the angel of death to pass over that house.**

8. How did the King respond to the tenth plague? (Ex 12:31-32)
    a. **He sent for Moses & Aaron and told them and the Israelites to get out (and take their goats, sheep, and cattle),**
    b. **To go worship their God, and**
    c. **To pray for a blessing for the King**

Chapter 27: The Ten Commandments

Supplemental Student Activities

1. What are the qualities of leadership? Discuss Moses as a human hero with positive and negative traits. Note how human our hero, Moses, is.
    a. List up to three negative character traits of Moses and one, big positive trait that came with the ten plagues.
    b. Negative character traits of Moses:
        i. Tries to get out of God's order
        ii. Lack of self confidence in public speaking
        iii. Lacks the courage to confront the King
    c. Positive character trait of Moses:
        i. Follows God's orders faithfully through the ten plagues
2. How do you handle your doubts & fears?
    a. Moses experiences fear, doubt, and concern when he considers the enormity of God's calling. Adolescents are often overwhelmed with the responsibilities of school, social life, and family obligations.
    b. Moses displays great courage when he approaches the King with a request to let the Israelites go free. Young people display courage when they move into the adult world and confront novel situations.
3. Discuss the themes in the Ten Commandments
    a. First three Commandments concern God.
    b. The other seven Commandments concern people.
    c. They are similar to Jesus' two commandments: Love God. Love your neighbor.
4. Interview a devoted, married couple or two very close friends. Ask them about the benefits and difficulties they experienced in their commitment to each other. What makes the relationship special? What do they each contribute to it?

Name: _____   Date: _____

Chapter 27: The Ten Commandments

1. Why did God not lead the Israelites by the Coastal Highway?
   _____
   _____

2. Why did the Israelites complain to Moses at the Red Sea?
   _____
   _____

3. Why did the Israelites complain to Moses and Aaron in the desert of Sin?
   _____

4. How did God provide food for them?
   _____

5. Where did Moses receive the Ten Commandments? _____

6. Who did the Israelites worship while Moses was gone for 40 days and nights?
   _____

7. Because the Israelites doubted and complained about Moses and God so much, how long did they wander in the desert become reaching Canaan?
   _____

8. Who did not reach the Promised land of Canaan? _____

Name: _____   Date: _____

Chapter 27: The Ten Commandments

1. Why did God not lead the Israelites by the Coastal Highway? (Ex 13:17)

   God was afraid they would return to Egypt if they had to fight the Egyptians or the Philistines.

2. Why did the Israelites complain to Moses at the Red Sea? (Ex 14:5-12)

   They complained because they were tired and hungry; and now the king had them trapped at the Red Sea and was about to slaughter them with 600 chariots

3. Why did the Israelites complain to Moses and Aaron in the desert of Sin? (Ex 16:3)

   They complained because they were starving.

4. How did God provide food for them? (Ex 16:4-16)

   God supplied the Israelites with meat (quail) in the evening and manna (bread) in the morning.

5. Where did Moses receive the Ten Commandments? (Ex 19:1-3, 20:1-17) **Mt. Sinai**

6. Who did the Israelites worship while Moses was gone for 40 days and nights? (Ex 32:1-4)

   A statue of a bull calf representing the god, El.

7. Because the Israelites doubted and complained about Moses and God so much, how long did they wander in the desert become reaching Canaan? (Numbers 14:26-34)

   40 years

8. Who did not reach the Promised land of Canaan? (Deuteronomy 34: 1-5) **Moses**

Crossword Puzzle Chapters 25-27

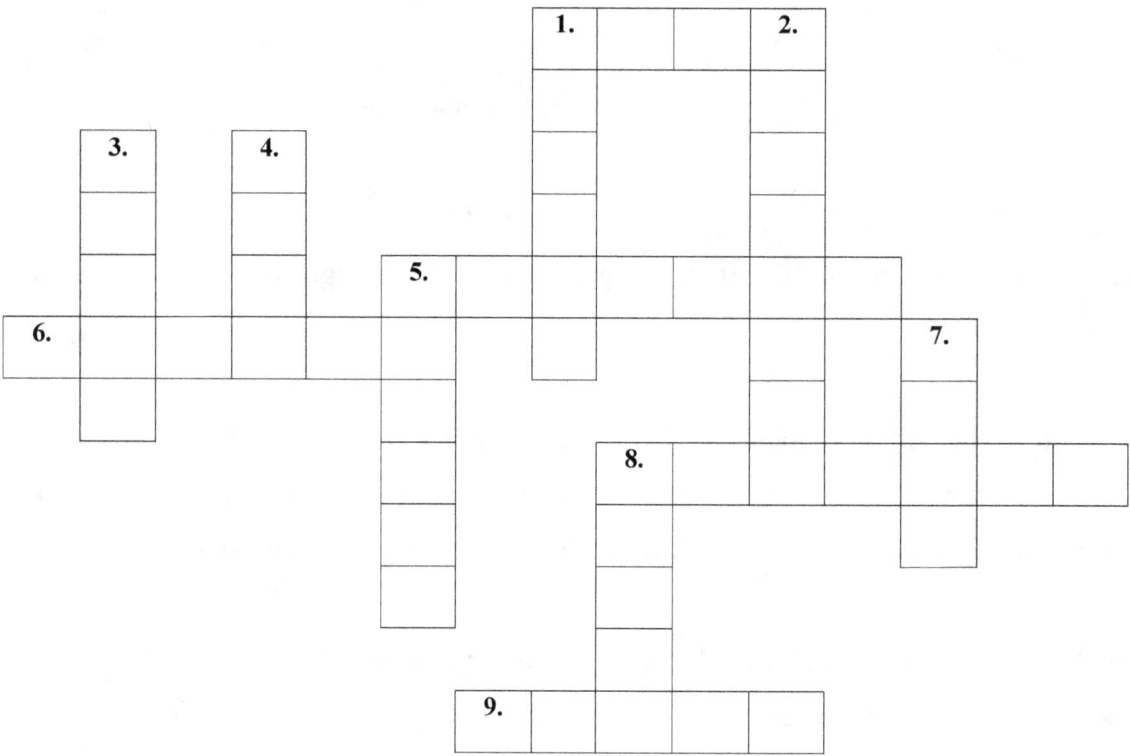

ACROSS:
1. Pellets of frozen rain
5. One who speaks divinely
6. A horizontal board above a door
8. A woman who helps with childbirth
9. A small game bird

DOWN:
1. Mint
2. Made with yeast; rises
3. A small plant shoot or twig
4. A very small, flying ins
5. An outbreak of disease
7. An inflamed, pus-filled swelling on the skin
8. Food substance (miraculously supplied to the Israelites)

Crossword Puzzle Chapters 25-27

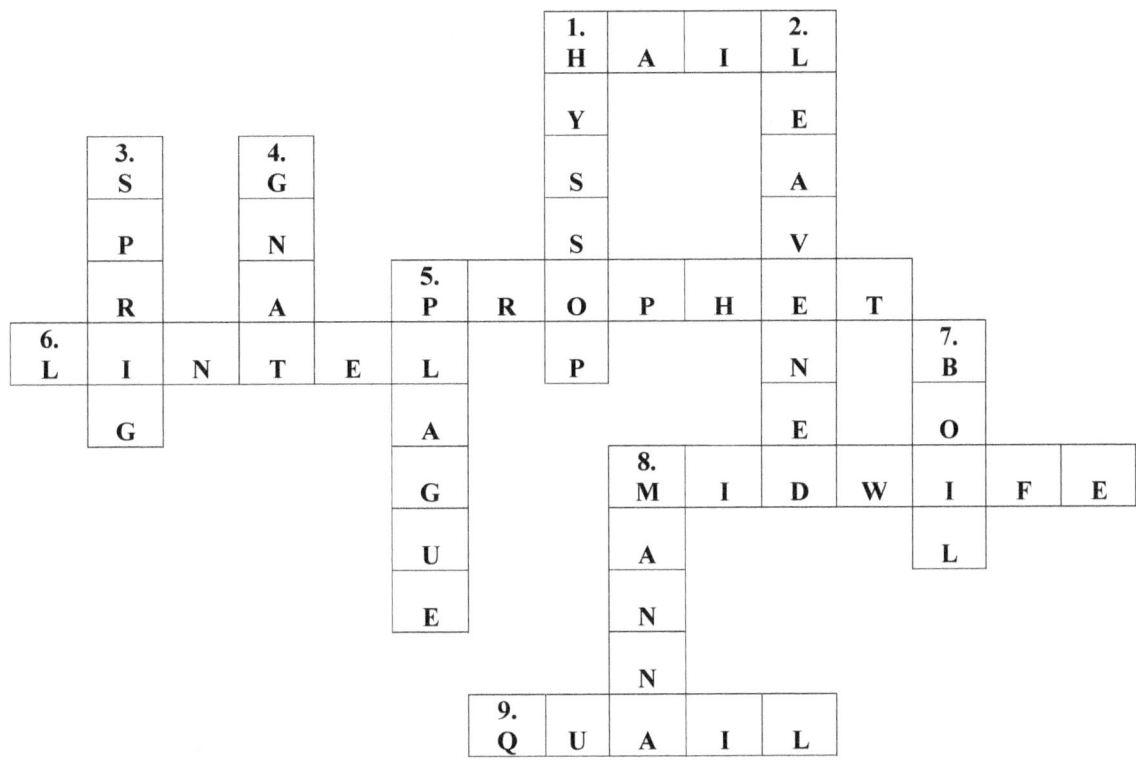

ACROSS:
1. Pellets of frozen rain
5. One who speaks divinely
6. A horizontal board above a door
8. A woman who helps with childbirth
9. A small game bird

DOWN:
1. Mint
2. Made with yeast; rises
3. A small plant shoot or twig
4. A very small, flying ins
5. An outbreak of disease
7. An inflamed, pus-filled swelling on the skin
8. Food substance (miraculously supplied to the Israelites)

Name: _____   Date: _____

Chapters 25-27: The Exodus Quiz

1. Why were the Israelites enslaved in Egypt? (i.e., 3 key reasons)

   _____
   _____
   _____

2. What did the Egyptians force the people of Israel to do?

   _____
   _____

3. What did the king of Egypt tell the Egyptian midwives to do?

   _____

4. Why did Moses kill the Egyptian?

   _____

5. Where did Moses flee to? _____

6. What did God promise to do for the Israelites in the story of Moses?
   a. Provide many descendants
   b. Provide pastureland
   c. Set them free
   d. Conquer the Egyptians

7. What was the first plague?
   a. Changed a staff into a snake
   b. Changed the water from the Nile to blood
   c. Covered the country with frogs
   d. Created swarms of flies

8. What was the last plague?
   a. Death of the animals
   b. Hail
   c. Locusts
   d. Death of the first born

(Over)

9. What animal was eaten on Passover?
   a. Fish
   b. Lamb
   c. Pork
   d. Chicken

10. What does Passover mean?
    a. The Angel of Death will pass over the homes of the Israelites who have marked their doors with a sign of blood and not kill their first-born sons.
    b. The Angel of Death will pass over the homes of all the first-born sons.
    c. The Angel of Death will pass over and bless all.
    d. The Angel of Death will kill all the first-born sons.

11. How did the king respond to the tenth plague?
    a. He told Moses and Aaron to get out.
    b. He told Moses and Aaron to get out, to worship their God, and to pray for a blessing for the king.
    c. He jailed Moses and Aaron.
    d. He chased them out of the country.

12. Why did God not lead the Israelites by way of the land of the Philistines?
    a. It was longer.
    b. It was more barren.
    c. It was easier for the Egyptians to catch them.
    d. They would have encountered warfare.

13. What did the King do after the Israelites left Egypt?
    a. He gave thanks to their God.
    b. He offered a sacrifice to their God.
    c. He changed his mind about letting them go and pursued them.
    d. He sent them food to speed their journey.

14. Where were the Israelites when the King caught up with them?
    a. Goshen
    b. Bitter Lakes
    c. Red Sea
    d. Marah

15. What effect did the miracle at the Red Sea (i.e., the parting of the sea and the drowning of the Egyptians) have on the Israelites?
    a. They complained less.
    b. They had faith in God and Moses.
    c. They complained to Aaron.
    d. They returned to Egypt.

(Over)

16. Where did Moses receive the Ten Commandments? _____

17. Who did not reach the Promised land of Canaan? _____

18. Plague means:
    a. an outbreak of disease
    b. very small flying bugs
    c. a sign
    d. an outbreak of the flu

19. Manna means:
    a. food miraculously supplied by the Lord
    b. rock
    c. a type of lamb
    d. unleavened bread

20. Leaven means:
    a. rises
    b. made with flour
    c. shrinks
    d. made with honey

I have neither given nor received any assistance on this quiz.

_____

Signature   Date

Name: _____   Date: _____

Chapters 25-27: The Exodus Quiz

1. Why were the Israelites enslaved in Egypt? (i.e., 3 key reasons)
   - **A new king who knew nothing about how Joseph came to power.**
   - **The Israelites were so numerous.**
   - **In case of war, they might join the enemy to fight**

2. What did the Egyptians force the people of Israel to do?

   The Egyptians forced them to build the cities of Pithom and Rameses as supply centers and later as slaves to construct buildings and working in their fields.

3. What did the king of Egypt tell the Egyptian midwives to do?

   The king commanded them to kill the baby Israelite boys and to let the baby girls live.

4. Why did Moses kill the Egyptian?

   Moses killed the Egyptian because the Egyptian had killed an Israelite.

5. Where did Moses flee to? **Midian**

6. What did God promise to do for the Israelites in the story of Moses?
   - a. Provide many descendants
   - b. Provide pastureland
   - **c. Set them free**
   - d. Conquer the Egyptians

7. What was the first plague?
   - a. Changed a staff into a snake
   - **b. Changed the water from the Nile to blood**
   - c. Covered the country with frogs
   - d. Created swarms of flies

8. What was the last plague?
   - a. Death of the animals
   - b. Hail
   - c. Locusts
   - **d. Death of the first born**

(Over)

9. What animal was eaten on Passover?
    a. Fish
    b. **Lamb**
    c. Pork
    d. Chicken

10. What does Passover mean?
    a. **The Angel of Death will pass over the homes of the Israelites who have marked their doors with a sign of blood and not kill their first-born sons.**
    b. The Angel of Death will pass over the homes of all the first-born sons.
    c. The Angel of Death will pass over and bless all.
    d. The Angel of Death will kill all the first-born sons.

11. How did the king respond to the tenth plague?
    a. He told Moses and Aaron to get out.
    b. **He told Moses and Aaron to get out, to worship their God, and to pray for a blessing for the king.**
    c. He jailed Moses and Aaron.
    d. He chased them out of the country.

12. Why did God not lead the Israelites by way of the land of the Philistines?
    a. It was longer.
    b. It was more barren.
    c. It was easier for the Egyptians to catch them.
    d. **They would have encountered warfare.**

13. What did the King do after the Israelites left Egypt?
    a. He gave thanks to their God.
    b. He offered a sacrifice to their God.
    c. **He changed his mind about letting them go and pursued them.**
    d. He sent them food to speed their journey.

14. Where were the Israelites when the King caught up with them?
    a. Goshen
    b. Bitter Lakes
    c. Red Sea
    d. Marah

15. What effect did the miracle at the Red Sea (i.e., the parting of the sea and the drowning of the Egyptians) have on the Israelites?
    a. They complained less.
    b. **They had faith in God and Moses.**
    c. They complained to Aaron.
    d. They returned to Egypt.

(Over)

16. Where did Moses receive the Ten Commandments? **Mt. Sinai**

17. Who did not reach the Promised land of Canaan? **Moses**

18. Plague means:
    c. **an outbreak of disease**
    d. very small flying bugs
    c. a sign
    d. an outbreak of the flu

19. Manna means:
    e. **food miraculously supplied by the Lord**
    f. rock
    g. a type of lamb
    h. unleavened bread

20. Leaven means:
    c. **rises**
    d. made with flour
    c. shrinks
    d. made with honey

I have neither given nor received any assistance on this quiz.

_____

Signature   Date

138

Name: _____   Date: _____

Chapter 28: Joshua

1. Who took over the leadership of Israel when Moses died? _____

2. What led the Israelites to the Jordan River and into the Promised Land?
   _____

3. What happened when the Israelite priests stepped into the river?
   _____

4. After the Israelites crossed the Jordan River, what did Joshua command the twelve men, one from each tribe, to do?
   _____

5. What was the purpose of the stones?
   _____
   _____

6. What happened after the priests left the riverbed? _____

7. What religious festival did the Israelites celebrate at Gilgal? _____

8. What change occurred in their food?
   _____

9. What instrument did the Israelites use to bring down the walls of Jericho? _____

Name: _____   Date: _____

Chapter 28: Joshua

1. Who took over the leadership of Israel when Moses died? (Joshua 1:1-6) **Joshua**

2. What led the Israelites to the Jordan River and into the Promised Land? (Joshua 3:3)
   The Covenant Box (aka Ark of the Covenant) led the people across the Jordan.

3. What happened when the Israelite priests stepped into the river? (Joshua 3:16)
   The river stopped flowing.

4. After the Israelites crossed the Jordan River, what did Joshua command the twelve men, one from each tribe, to do? (Joshua 4:3)
   They were to select a stone from the riverbed and carry it to their camp that night.

5. What was the purpose of the stones? (Joshua 4:6-7)
   The stones were to build a memorial to remind the Israelites what God had done that day for them in crossing the Jordan River.

6. What happened after the priests left the riverbed? (Joshua 4:18)
   The river resumed flowing again.

7. What religious festival did the Israelites celebrate at Gilgal? (Joshua 5:10-11)
   They celebrated their first Passover in the Promised Land.

8. What change occurred in their food? (Joshua 5:11-12)
   For the first time, they ate food locally grown in Canaan. The manna stopped arriving.

9. What instrument did the Israelites use to bring down the walls of Jericho? (Joshua 6:3-5)
   Trumpets

Name: _____   Date: _____

Chapter 29: Judges

1. Describe the three functions of a judge:
    a. _____
    b. _____
    c. _____

2. What actions by Israelites helped to them forget God's laws and worship other gods?
    a. _____
    b. _____

3. When the Israelites strayed from God, what happened?
   _____

4. What happened when the Israelites repented? (See Cycle of the Israelites in the story above.)
   _____

5. Who was the famous woman judge? _____

6. Which judge refused to be the ruler of the Israelites? _____

7. How did the Philistines bring down Samson?
   _____
   _____
   _____

8. How did Samson avenge (take vengeance for) his actions and the Philistines?
   _____
   _____

9. List each of the cycles of the Israelites and briefly describe each cycle.
    a. _____
    b. _____
    c. _____
    d. _____

Name: _____ Date: _____

Chapter 29: Judges

1. Describe the three functions of a judge: (See the Ch. 29 story, Introduction to Judges)
    a. **Unite the tribes in a common defense**
    b. **Restore the faith in their one God**
    c. **Resolve disputes**

2. What actions by Israelites helped them to forget God's laws and worship other gods? (Ch. 29, 3rd paragraph)
    a. **Offering sacrifices to the fertility gods Baal and Astarte for better crops**
    b. **Marrying non-Israelites and being tempted to worship their gods**

3. When the Israelites strayed from God, what happened? (Ch. 29 story, 4th paragraph)
Military defeats occurred.

4. What happened when the Israelites repented? (See Ch. 29, Deborah or Notes, Cycle of the Israelites)
God would send a leader, a judge, to lead them temporarily in military and religious matters.

5. Who was the famous woman judge? (Judge 4:4) **Deborah**

6. Which judge refused to be the ruler of the Israelites? (Judges 8:22-23) **Gideon**

7. How did the Philistines bring down Samson? (Judges 16:4-22)
Five Philistine kings kept pressuring Delilah to find out why Samson is so strong. They offered her eleven hundred pieces of silver each. She kept asking Samson until finally in a weak moment he told her.

8. How did Samson avenge (take vengeance for) his actions and the Philistines? (Judges 16:28-30)
While chained to the columns he pulled them together and caused the roof to collapse killing him and more Philistines than he had ever killed before.

9. In the Book of Judges, we notice a pattern known as the cycle of the Israelites. List each of the cycles and briefly describe each cycle. (See Notes, Cycle of the Israelites)
    a. **Sin – idol worship (e.g., Baal and Astartes)**
    b. **Punishment – military defeats (e.g., by the Philistines)**
    c. **Repentance – Israelites request forgiveness from God**
    d. **Forgiveness – God's assistance (new judge appointed to lead the Israelites militarily and religiously)**

Name: _____   Date: _____

Chapter 30: Ruth

1. Why did Naomi and her husband leave Bethlehem and go to Moab?
   _____

2. How did Ruth respond when her mother-in-law (Naomi) told her to return to her people? Quote directly from the story.
   _____
   _____

3. Why did Ruth go to Bethlehem with Naomi?
   _____

4. How did clans take care of unfortunate members?
   _____
   _____

5. Why was Boaz so impressed with Ruth?
   _____

6. How would you describe Ruth? Use at least 3 adjectives.
   _____

7. What important Old Testament person was descended from Ruth? _____

8. Define glean. _____

9. Define Gentile. _____

Name: _____   Date: _____

Chapter 30: Ruth

1. Why did Naomi and her husband leave Bethlehem and go to Moab? (Ruth 1:1-2)
    They left Bethlehem due to a severe drought.

2. How did Ruth respond when her mother-in-law (Naomi) told her to return to her people? Quote directly from the story. (Ruth 1:16)
    "Wherever you go, I will go; wherever you live, I will live. Your people shall be my people; and your God will be my God." (Ruth 1:16) (GNT)

3. Why did Ruth go to Bethlehem with Naomi? (Ruth 1:16-18)
    Ruth was determined to take care of Naomi.

4. How did clans take care of unfortunate members? (See the Ch. 30 story.)
    They let the widows and others glean the fields (i.e., follow the workers and pick up any grain left behind).

5. Why was Boaz so impressed with Ruth? (See the Ch. 30 story. Also Ruth 2:11-12)
    He was impressed he was that she would leave her people to care for her mother-in-law.

6. How would you describe Ruth? Use at least 3 adjectives.
    Caring, loving, kind, devoted, etc.

7. What important Old Testament person was descended from Ruth? (Ruth 4:17) **David**

8. Define glean. **To pick up grain left behind**

9. Define Gentile. **A non-Israelite; non-Jew.**

Crossword Puzzle Chapters 28-30

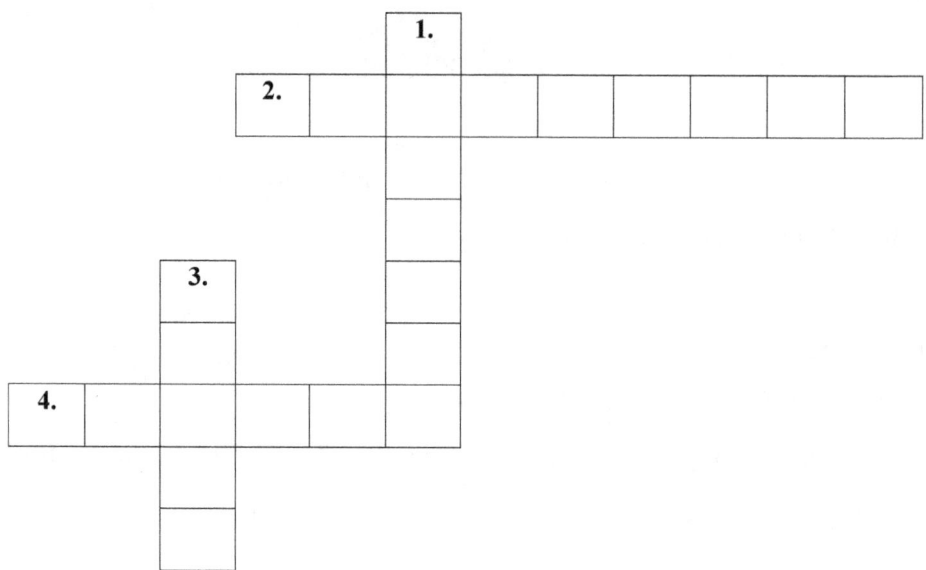

ACROSS:
2. A government by officials regarded as divinely inspired
4. Take retaliation for

DOWN:
1. A non-Israelite; a non-Jew
3. Pick up grain left behind

Crossword Puzzle Chapters 28-30

		1. G				
2. T	H	E	O	C	R	A	C	Y
		N				
		T				
	3. G		I			
	L		L			
4. A	V	E	N	G	E	
	A					
	N					

ACROSS:
2. A government by officials regarded as divinely inspired
4. Take retaliation for

DOWN:
1. A non-Israelite; a non-Jew
3. Pick up grain left behind

Name: _____ Date: _____

Chapters 28-30: The Joshua-Judges-Ruth Quiz

1. What led the Israelites to the Jordan River and into the promised Land??
    a. The Covenant Box
    b. Their flag
    c. Abraham
    d. Their troops

2. What was the major sin of the Israelites in the Book of the Judges?
    a. They worshipped other gods.
    b. They failed to pay taxes.
    c. They conquered native tribes.
    d. They enslaved others.

3. Which of the following was not a function of an Israelite judge?
    a. Defend Israel against its enemies
    b. Rule the Israelites
    c. Settle tribal disputes
    d. Call the Israelites back to God

4. Which of the following was not one of the four cycles of the Israelites?
    a. Sin- idol worship
    b. Repentance- Israelite request for forgiveness
    c. Offerings- Israelite sacrifices of lambs and goats to God
    d. Punishment- military defeats

5. Who was the famous woman judge?
    a. Ruth
    b. Rachel
    c. Naomi
    d. Deborah

6. Gideon
    a. commanded over 900 chariots
    b. agreed to fight Sisera when Deborah went with him
    c. helped Samson defeat the Philistines
    d. refused to serve as the ruler of the Israelites

7. Samson…
    a. refused to tell his secret
    b. never lost his eyesight
    c. used his regained strength to pull down the columns of the temple, killing himself and numerous Philistines
    d. kept his head clean-shaven

(Over)

8. Who among the following was not an Israelite judge?
    a. Deborah
    b. Gideon
    c. Delilah
    d. Samson

9. Who said, "Wherever you go, I will go. Wherever you live, I will live. Your people will be my people. And your God will be my God."
    a. Deborah
    b. Gideon
    c. Ruth
    d. Samson

10. What does glean mean?
    a. to pick up grain left behind
    b. type of grain
    c. bright
    d. altar

11. What does Gentile mean?
    a. a high priest
    b. a non-Israelite
    c. temple
    d. polytheistic

I have neither given nor received any assistance on this quiz.

_____

Signature   Date

Name: _____   Date: _____

Chapters 28-30: The Joshua-Judges-Ruth Quiz

1. What led the Israelites to the Jordan River and into the promised Land??
   - **a. The Covenant Box**
   - b. Their flag
   - c. Abraham
   - d. Their troops

2. What was the major sin of the Israelites in the Book of the Judges?
   - **a. They worshipped other gods.**
   - b. They failed to pay taxes.
   - c. They conquered native tribes.
   - d. They enslaved others.

3. Which of the following was not a function of an Israelite judge?
   - a. Defend Israel against its enemies
   - **b. Rule the Israelites**
   - c. Settle tribal disputes
   - d. Call the Israelites back to God

4. Which of the following was not one of the four cycles of the Israelites?
   - a. Sin- idol worship
   - b. Repentance- Israelite request for forgiveness
   - **c. Offerings- Israelite sacrifices of lambs and goats to God**
   - d. Punishment- military defeats

5. Who was the famous woman judge?
   - a. Ruth
   - b. Rachel
   - c. Naomi
   - **d. Deborah**

6. Gideon
   - a. commanded over 900 chariots
   - b. agreed to fight Sisera when Deborah went with him
   - c. helped Samson defeat the Philistines
   - **d. refused to serve as the ruler of the Israelites**

7. Samson…
   - a. refused to tell his secret
   - b. never lost his eyesight
   - **c. used his regained strength to pull down the columns of the temple, killing himself and numerous Philistines**
   - d. kept his head clean-shaven

(Over)

8. Who among the following was not an Israelite judge?
   a. Deborah
   c. Delilah
   b. Gideon
   d. Samson

9. Who said, "Wherever you go, I will go. Wherever you live, I will live. Your people will be my people. And your God will be my God."
   a. Deborah
   c. Ruth
   b. Gideon
   d. Samson

10. What does glean mean?
    a. to **pick up grain left behind**
    c. bright
    b. type of grain
    d. altar

11. What does Gentile mean?
    a. a high priest
    c. temple
    b. a non-Israelite
    d. polytheistic

I have neither given nor received any assistance on this quiz.

_____
Signature   Date

Chapter 31: Samuel

Supplemental Student Discussion

1. What is God's message in selecting Saul as the first king?
    a. All of us are important, including those from the smallest tribe and least important family!

2. Where have we seen this type of reaction before? "I belong to the tribe of Benjamin, the smallest tribe in Israel, and my family is the least important one of the tribe. Why, then, do you talk to me like this?" (Chapter 31) (1 Samuel 9:21) (GNT)
    a. Moses: I am nobody. How can I go to the king and bring the Israelites out of Egypt?" "No, Lord, don't send me. I have never been a good speaker…I am a poor speaker, slow and hesitant." (Ex 3:11, 4:10) (GNT)
    b. Gideon: "How can I rescue Israel? My clan is the weakest in the tribe of Manasseh, and I am the least important member of my family." (judges 6:15) (GNT)

3. Identify and explain the impact of the two major problems that the Israelites were having: religion and government.
    a. Religion. The Israelites were not completely faithful to their new, monotheistic religion. They fell to the temptation to worship the fertility gods, Baal and Ashtoreth, and then suffered military defeats. However, excavation evidence did reveal that they followed some of their new religion's practices, namely the avoidance of pork.
    b. Government. The Israelites were not as efficient as their neighbors with standing armies under a single leader, a king. The Israelites had to convince each tribe to raise troops each time they were threatened or attacked.

Summary Outline: 1st Book of Samuel

Need for Unity: Judges 21:25 – "There was no king in Israel at that time. Everyone did whatever they pleased."

Background:
- The Book of Samuel reports the transition from judges to kings
- Principal leaders:
    - Samuel – the last of the great Judges
    - Saul – Israel's first king
    - David – Saul's successor
    - Solomon – Israel's third king
- Written while Israelites were in exile in Babylon
- Based on several written sources no longer available
- Author unknown

Theme:
- Faithfulness to God brings success
- Disobedience brings disaster

Timeline:
- Occurred 1000 BC
- Written 600 BC

Problems:
- Government – The 12 tribes of Israel would unite behind a leader (judge) for military protection when necessary. When the crisis was over, the judge returned to his/her previous occupation.
- Religion – Israelite tribes sometimes worshiped other gods. God punished Israel by not protecting them from attacks by the Philistines.

Name: _____   Date: _____

Chapter 31: Samuel

1. Who were the Canaanite fertility god and goddess? _____ _____

2. Where were ancient towns typically located? _____

3. Describe a typical Israelite house.
   _____
   _____
   _____
   _____

4. In this area of the world who believed in an afterlife and who may not have believed?
   _____
   _____

5. What is the First Book of Samuel about?
   _____

6. Who frequently threatened the Israelites?
   _____

7. Were Samuel's sons like their father? Explain your answer.
   _____
   _____
   _____

(Over)

8. Why did the Israelites want a king to govern them? List two reasons.

9. How did Samuel say a king might treat them? Give four specific examples.

10. How did Saul react to being selected to be the king of the Israelites?

11. Where have we seen this type of reaction before?

Name: _____   Date: _____

Chapter 31: Samuel

1. Who were the Canaanite fertility god and goddess? (See Ch. 31 story, Overview…) **Baal and Ashtoreth**

2. Where were ancient towns typically located? (See Ch. 31 story, Life…) **On the top of a small hill or tell**

3. Describe a typical Israelite house. (See Ch. 31 story, Life…)
The typical house was built on a stone base with mudbrick walls and a flat roof which was a cool place to sleep in the hot weather. Israelite houses typically had three to four rooms built around a small courtyard: a stable for animals, a central storage area, a living space, and sleeping quarters. The house would also have cisterns to collect water.

4. In this area of the world who believed in an afterlife and who may not have believed? (See Ch. 31 story, Life…, #3. Death)
The Egyptians and Mesopotamians believed in an afterlife but there is little evidence that the Israelites did before their exile.

5. What is the First Book of Samuel about? (See Ch. 31 story, Introduction)
It describes the transition from judges to a monarchy.

6. Who frequently threatened the Israelites? (See Ch. 31 story, Introduction)
The "sea people," the Philistines

7. Were Samuel's sons like their father? Explain your answer. (1 Samuel 2:12-17; 8:1-3)
No. They were scoundrels who did not follow the temple's rules. They disrespected the offerings people brought and thus insulted God. They took food offered as sacrifices when they should not have. They slept with women who worked at the entrance to the temple. They accepted bribes and did not decide cases fairly.

8. Why did the Israelites want a king to govern them? List two reasons. (1 Samuel 8:1-3,19-20)

    They wanted a king because they did not want Samuel's corrupt sons to become their leaders. They wanted a king like other countries.

9. How did Samuel say a king might treat them? Give four specific examples. (1 Samuel 8:11-17)

    - **He will make soldiers of your sons. Some will be chariots; others will march on foot;**
    - **Some will be officers in charge of a thousand men while others in charge of fifty men.**
    - **Your sons will have to plow his fields, harvest his crops, and make his weapons and the equipment.**
    - **Your daughters will have to make perfumes for him and cook for him.**
    - **The king will take your best fields, olive groves, and vineyards for his use and for his officials.**
    - **He will need your servants and best cattle and donkeys to work for him.**
    - **He will take a tenth of your flock.**

10. How did Saul react to being selected to be the king of the Israelites? (1 Samuel 9:21)

    Saul was surprised. He said he belonged to the smallest tribe and the least important family. "I belong to the tribe of Benjamin, the smallest tribe in Israel, and my family is the least important one of the tribe. Why, then, do you talk to me like this?" (1 Samuel 9:21) (GNT)

11. Where have we seen this type of reaction before? (Ch. 25, p. 107-108) (Ch. 29, p. 134)
    - **Moses: "I am nobody. How can I go to the king and bring the Israelites out of Egypt?" "No, Lord, don't send me. I have never been a good speaker." (Exodus 3:11 & 4:10) (GNT)**
    - **Gideon: "But Lord, how can I rescue Israel? My clan is the weakest in the tribe of Manasseh and I am the least important member of my family." (Judges 6:15) (GNT)**

Chapter 32: Saul

Supplemental Consideration/Discussion
1. What do you think is the message in God's loss of confidence in Saul?
    a. Be faithful in following God's commands

2. Do you think God was fair?
    a. Yes. Saul did not follow directions. He was not a strong leader with his people. This could have been a bigger problem in another situation.
    b. No. These were minor issues. Saul used his judgment which seemed reasonable given the circumstances.

3. How would you describe Saul?
    a. Unfaithful. Anxious. Influenced by others. Did not fully trust God. Inconsistent. Tried hard.

Name: _____   Date: _____

Chapter 32: Saul

1. Twice Saul did not follow God's directions as told by Samuel. What did Saul fail to do?

    a. _____
    _____

    b. _____
    _____

2. What was the name of Saul's son who fought along with his father? _____

3. What was God's reaction to Saul's failures?
    _____

4. How did God decide which person was to be a king?
    _____
    _____
    _____
    _____

5. How did Saul's staff treat his illness?
    _____

Name: _____   Date: _____

Chapter 32: Saul

1. Twice Saul did not follow God's directions as told by Samuel. What did Saul fail to do? (1 Samuel 13:5-14; 1 Samuel 15:1-9)

    a. **At Gilgal, Saul went ahead without Samuel and offered a sacrifice to the God.**

    b. **Saul spared the life of the Amalekite king and of his best sheep and cattle.**

2. What was the name of Saul's son who fought along with his Father? (1 Samuel 13:1)

    Jonathan

3. What was God's reaction to Saul's failures? (1 Samuel 13:13-14; 1 Samuel 15:10-11, 22-23)

    God was not pleased that Saul did not obey his/her commands as transmitted through Samuel. God sent Samuel to anoint David as the next king.

4. How did God decide which person was to be a king? (1 Samuel 16:7)

    1 Samuel 16:7: But God said to him, "Pay no attention to how tall and handsome he is. I have rejected him, because I do not judge as people judge. They look at the outward appearance, but I look at the heart." (1 Samuel 16:7) (GNT)

5. How did Saul's staff treat his illness? (1 Samuel 16:16-18)

    They sent an attendant to fetch Jesse's son David who was known as a good musician. Whenever Saul was down, David would play his harp and cheer up Saul.

Chapter 33: Young David

Supplemental Student Activities

1. In their celebration the women sang, "Saul has killed thousands, but David tens of thousands." Saul did not like this, and he became very angry. He said, "For David they claim tens of thousands but only thousands for me. They will be making him king next!" And so, he was jealous and suspicious of David from that day on. (1 Samuel 18: 7-9) (GNT) How could Saul have better handled his jealousy?

Among the possible answers:

a. Learn to appreciate others' success.

b. Learn to accept oneself for what he/she is and not compare one aspect of oneself to others for we are each different and complicated.

c. Consider the anger management options for Cain: discuss what would work best for the two of them.

2. Discuss the story of the David and Jonathan's friendship: Consider reading and discussing the following Bible verses: 1 Samuel 18:1-5 and 1 Samuel 20:1-42

Name: _____   Date: _____

Chapter 33: Young David

1. Describe the ancient world concept of single combat.
   _____
   _____
   _____

2. What did Saul promise the soldier who could defeat Goliath?
   _____
   _____

3. Explain why David thought he could beat Goliath.
   _____
   _____

4. Why did Saul's feelings about David change?
   _____
   _____

5. Why is Jonathan considered a model of friendship?
   _____
   _____
   _____

6. Why did Saul present David with Michal, his daughter?
   _____
   _____
   _____

(Over)

7. How did Saul attempt to kill David? Describe 3 attempts.

   _____

   _____

   _____

8. How did Jonathan help David with the New Moon Festival? What was Saul's reaction? Summarize in your own words.

   _____

   _____

   _____

9. Why did David not kill Saul when he had an opportunity?

   _____

10. What evidence did David offer Saul of his innocence of treason or wrongdoing?

    _____

    _____

11. How did Saul react to David's words?

    _____

Name: _____ Date: _____

Chapter 33: Young David

1. Describe the ancient world concept of single combat. (See Ch. 33 story, Goliath)

   To avoid widespread bloodshed, a combatant would challenge to the other side to put up one combatant to fight a duel, typically until the death of one of them. The fight would occur on the open ground between the two opposing armies.

2. What did Saul promise the soldier who could defeat Goliath? (1 Samuel 17:25)

   He would receive the king's daughter in marriage.
   Saul would free his father's family from taxes.

3. Explain why David thought he could beat Goliath. (1 Samuel 17:34-37)

   He had killed lions and bears before (presumably with his sling and shot).
   God had saved him before; God will save him again.

4. Why did Saul's feelings about David change? (1 Samuel 18:7-9)

   Saul became angry and then jealous of David's popularity.
   He thought they might make David the king.

5. Why is Jonathan considered a model of friendship? (1 Samuel 18:1-4; 19:1-7; 20:1-42; 23:14-18)

   David and Jonathan became very close friends. Jonathan shared his clothes with David. Jonathan dealt with his father's jealousy of David. Jonathan sided with David over his father. In the ultimate test of friendship, Jonathan risked his life for David.

6. Why did Saul present David with Michal, his daughter? (1 Samuel 18:20-25)

   Saul planned to use Michal to trap David. He offered Michal to David in marriage if he would first kill a hundred Philistines. Saul thought the Philistines would surely kill him this time. **(Over)**

7. How did Saul attempt to kill David? Describe 3 attempts. (1 Samuel 18:11, 13, 25; 19:10-11)

   He threw a spear at David twice.

   He asked David to fight another battle with the Philistines.

   He asked David to kill 100 Philistines in order to marry his daughter, Michal.

   He sent men to David's house to kill him.

8. How did Jonathan help David with the New Moon Festival? What was Saul's reaction? Summarize in your own words.

   (1 Samuel 20:1-34)

   Jonathan explained David's absence from the palace festival as a need to visit his own family in Bethlehem for their New Moon festival. In anger Saul threw a spear at his own son accusing him of siding with David.

9. Why did David not kill Saul when he had an opportunity? (1 Samuel 24:6)

   David did not kill Saul out of respect for God who chose Saul as his king.

10. What evidence did David offer Saul of his innocence of treason or wrongdoing? (1 Samuel 24:11)

    David said the fact that he cut a piece of Saul's robe off instead of killing him was proof of his good intentions.

11. How did Saul react to David's words? (1 Samuel 24:16-19)

    He cried and said, "You are right, and I am wrong. You have been good to me, while I have been wrong to you!...How often does someone catch an enemy and let him go away unharmed?" (1 Samuel 24:17,19) (GNT)

Chapter 34: David's Reign

Supplemental Student Question

1. Identify three reasons to select Jerusalem as the capital of Israel.
    a. Its location did not favor any of the twelve tribes. None had occupied it.
    b. It was centrally located in the new kingdom.
    c. It was at the crossroads of two trading routes making it ideal for governing and conducting business.

Overview: 2nd Book of Samuel

Nationhood Revisited
    Advantages
- Strong military leadership for protection
- Strong religious leadership to avoid temptations

    Disadvantages
- Power struggles
- Turning away from God

Principal Leaders
- Samuel – the last of the great judges
- Saul – Israel's first king
- David – Saul's successor, a nation builder
- Solomon – Israel's third king, a temple builder

Name: _____   Date: _____

Chapter 34: David's Reign

1. Where was David's first capital? _____

2. What was it the capital of? _____

3. When Judah and Israel combined, where did David make the capital? _____

4. How did David conquer Jerusalem?
   _____
   _____

5. What sacred object did David bring into Jerusalem? _____

6. What is the Davidic Covenant?
   _____
   _____

7. Who was Bathsheba?
   _____

8. How did David arrange for Uriah to be killed?
   _____
   _____

9. Following Uriah's death, what did David do with Bathsheba?
   _____

10. Who was Nathan? _____

   (Over)

11. Then, what did God do about David's actions?
   _____

12. What was the type of short story that Nathan told David? _____

13. How did David react?
   _____

14. What did David and Bathsheba name their second son? _____

Name: _____   Date: _____

Chapter 34: David's Reign

1. Where was David's first capital? (2 Samuel 2:4)   **Hebron**

2. What was it the capital of? (2 Samuel 2:4) **The tribe of Judah in the southern part of Israel**

3. When Judah and Israel combined, where did David make the capital? (2 Samuel 5:5) **Jerusalem**

4. How did David conquer Jerusalem? (2 Samuel 5:6-8)
   He sneaked through the water tunnel serving Jerusalem and then mounted a surprise attack from within the city.

5. What sacred object did David bring into Jerusalem? (2 Samuel 6:12) **The Covenant Box**

6. What is the Davidic Covenant? (2 Samuel 7:16)
   God's promise to David that he will always have descendants, and that God will make his kingdom last forever. His dynasty will never end.

7. Who was Bathsheba? (2 Samuel 11:3)
   She was the wife of Uriah, an officer in David's army.

8. How did David arrange for Uriah to be killed? (2 Samuel 11:15)
   He had Uriah moved to the center of the front line where the fighting will be the heaviest.

9. Following Uriah's death, what did David do with Bathsheba? (2 Samuel 11:27)
   He married Bathsheba.

10. Who was Nathan? (2 Samuel 12:1) **He was a prophet.**

    (Over)

11. Then, what did God do about David's actions? (2 Samuel 12:1-7, 10)
    God sent the prophet, Nathan, to tell David a parable (i.e., to make him see the evil he had done) of a rich man and a poor man.

12. What was the type of short story that Nathan told David? (Ch. 34, p. 164, Nathan's Message)
    A parable.

13. How did David react? (2 Samuel 12:13)
    David immediately repented and said he had sinned against God.

15. What did David and Bathsheba name their second son? (2 Samuel 12:24) **Solomon.**

Chapter 35: David's Sons

Supplemental Student Activity

1. Discuss how David is not a perfect hero.
    a. Falls in love with a married woman
    b. Orders her husband, Uriah, to the front lines so he will be killed in battle
    c. Is a poor father with out of control sons

Name: _____   Date: _____

Chapter 35: David's Sons
An Out of Control Son!

1. David was successful as a _____ and a _____ but a failure as a _____

2. David's second son _____ ordered his slaves to _____ his brother, _____ because
   _____
   _____

3. What did David do after hearing about Absalom's revolt?
   _____

4. What did Joab do with Absalom when he found him in a tree?
   _____

5. How did David react to the news about Absalom?
   _____

6. What did Joab finally convince David to do?
   _____

Name: _____   Date: _____

Chapter 35: David's Sons
An Out of Control Son!

1. David was successful as a **warrior king**, but a failure as a **father**. (See Ch. 35 story, David Is Not a Perfect Hero)

2. David's second son, **Absalom**, ordered his slaves to **kill** his brother, **Amnon**, because **Amnon was next in line to be king and Absalom was second in line. Absalom wanted to be the next king.** (2 Samuel 13:26-29) (See Ch. 35 story, David Is Not a Perfect Hero & A Murder in the Family)

3. What did David do after hearing about Absalom's revolt? (2 Samuel 15:14)
   David and his family left Jerusalem.

4. What did Joab do with Absalom when he found him in a tree? (2 Samuel 18:14-15)
   Without a moment's thought, he thrust his spear into Absalom three times killing him.

5. How did David react to the news about Absalom? (2 Samuel 18:32-33) (See Ch. 35 story, A Death in the Family)
   He was stricken with grief. He stayed in his room for days.

6. What did Joab finally convince David to do? (2 Samuel 19:5-8)
   Joab convinced David to thank the troops.

Name: _____ Date: _____

Chapter 36: Solomon

1. Who tried unsuccessfully to succeed David as the king of Israel? _____

2. How long did David rule Israel? _____

3. What did Solomon ask God for?
   _____

4. Solomon was a very wealthy man. Give some examples of his wealth.
   a. _____
   b. _____
   _____
   c. _____

5. List examples of Solomon's wisdom.
   a. _____
   b. _____
   c. _____

6. What practical circumstances prevented David from building a temple in Solomon's opinion?
   _____
   _____

(Over)

7. How did Solomon assign the Israelites to work in Lebanon? (In other words, what was their work schedule?)

   _____
   _____

8. How long did it take to build the temple? _____

9. What impressed the Queen of Sheba about Solomon?

   _____
   _____
   _____

10. How was Solomon unfaithful?
    a. _____
    b. _____

11. Describe what happened to the Kingdom of Israel after Solomon's death.

   _____
   _____
   _____

Name: _____   Date: _____

Chapter 36: Solomon

1. Who tried unsuccessfully to succeed David as the king of Israel? (1 Kings 1:5-6)
   Adonijah

2. How long did David rule Israel? (1 Kings 2:11) **40 years**

3. What did Solomon ask God for? (1 Kings 3:9)
   Wisdom to rule his people justly

4. Solomon was a very wealthy man. Give some examples of his wealth. (1 Kings 4:21-26)
   a. **He had 12,000 cavalry horses and 40,000 chariot horses.**
   b. **He expanded the kingdom to include all the nations from the Euphrates River to Egypt.**
   c. **The conquered nations paid a tribute (tax) to him.**

5. List additional examples of Solomon's wisdom. (1 Kings 4:32-34)
   a. **He wrote as many as 3,000 proverbs.**
   b. **He wrote as many as 1,000 songs.**
   c. **He was knowledgeable about the plant and animal world.**

6. What practical circumstances prevented David from building a temple in Solomon's opinion? (1 Kings 5:3)
   David was constantly fighting wars to establish the kingdom of Israel in Canaan.

(Over)

7. How did Solomon assign the Israelites to work in Lebanon? (In other words, what was their work schedule?) (1 Kings 5:13-14)

   Solomon forced 30,000 Israelite men to work one month every three months, 10,000 men at a time.

8. How long did it take to build the temple? (1 Kings 6:38) **Seven years**

9. What impressed the Queen of Sheba about Solomon? (1 Kings 10:2-5)

   She was impressed with his wisdom, his wealth, his beautiful palace, his well-organized staff, and the sacrifices he offered in the temple.

10. How was Solomon unfaithful? (1 Kings 11:1-8)

    a. **He married foreign women. They were polytheistic.**

    b. **He worshipped foreign gods and built places of worship to foreign gods.**

11. Describe what happened to the Kingdom of Israel after Solomon's death. (1 Kings 12:1-20)

    The northern tribes revolted because they resented the forced labor and heavy taxes. Jeroboam became the king of the northern tribes called Israel. Solomon's son, Rehoboam, became the king of Judah.

Crossword Puzzle Chapters 31-37

ACROSS:
2. A musical string instrument on a triangular frame
5. A mournful cry
6. Transition from mother's milk to food; free from dependence
7. Payment made by a state to a ruler that shows dependence
8. A mound formed by the accumulated remains of ancient settlements

DOWN:
1. A short story with a moral lesson
3. A royal staff used as a symbol of authority
4. Apply oil in a sacred rite

Crossword Puzzle Chapters 31-37

							1. P		
						2. H	A	R	P
	3. S						R		
	C		4. A			5. W	A	I	L
6. W	E	A	N				B		
	P		O				L		
	7. T	R	I	B	U	T	E		
	E		N						
	R		8. T	E	L	L			

ACROSS:
2. A musical string instrument on a triangular frame
5. A mournful cry
6. Transition from mother's milk to food; free from dependence
7. Payment made by a state to a ruler that shows dependence
8. A mound formed by the accumulated remains of ancient settlements

DOWN:
1. A short story with a moral lesson
3. A royal staff used as a symbol of authority
4. Apply oil in a sacred rite

Name: _____   Date: _____

Chapters 31-36: Samuel, Saul, David & Solomon Quiz

Please identify each speaker of the following quotes:

1. "Choose one of your men to fight me. If he wins and kills me, we will be your slaves, but if I win and kill him, you will be our slaves."

   _____

2. "I have killed lions and bears, and I will do the same to this heathen Philistine, who has defied the army of the living God."

   _____

3. "You are right, and I am wrong. You have been so good to me, while I have done such wrong to you! How often does someone catch an enemy and then let him go away unharmed?"

   _____

5. Samuel is…
   a. the last of the great judges   c. Saul's successor
   b. Israel's first king   d. Joshua's son

6. Which of the following was <u>not</u> a reason the Israelites wanted a king?
   a. To unite the twelve tribes of Israel for military protection
   b. To keep all the Israelite tribes faithful to God's covenant and Ten Commandments
   c. To defend Israel from attacks by other nations such as the Philistines
   d. To raise money for a temple

7. Which of the following was <u>not</u> one of Samuel's warnings about how a king might treat the Israelites?
   a. A king will make soldiers of your sons.
   b. A king will make your sons plow his fields.
   c. A king will make your daughters work as his cooks.
   d. A king will impose taxes on trade.

   (Over)

8. What was God's theme in selecting Saul and David?
    a. Membership in the best tribes was important.
    b. Membership in the best families was important.
    c. The smallest and least appealing was important, too.
    d. Appearance was important.

9. Why did Saul present David with Michal for marriage?
    a. He was to be David's servant.
    b. He was to be one of David's officers in the military.
    c. She was to be David's servant.
    d. He planned to use her to trap David into fighting the Philistines and hopefully die in battle.

10. Who was Jonathan?
    a. Saul's son-in-law
    b. A close friend of David's
    c. Samuel's son
    d. Ahimelech's son

11. Why was David unable to kill Saul?
    a. Because he could not catch him
    b. Because Saul outnumbered him
    c. Because Saul was still God's chosen king
    d. Because Saul was stronger

12. Which of the following is not a reason to select Jerusalem as the capital of Israel:
    a. A great conquest/victory.
    b. Jerusalem did not belong to any of the 12 tribes of Israel.
    c. The selection of Jerusalem did not favor any of the 12 tribes
    d. Jerusalem was ideally located between the northern and southern tribes of Israel.

13. How did David's men infiltrate Jerusalem?
    a. His men disguised themselves as traders.
    b. His men hid in nearby fields until nighttime.
    c. His men entered through the water tunnel.
    d. His men hid in scattered houses in Jerusalem until the time of attack.

14. What sacred object did David bring to Jerusalem?
    a. an altar
    b. his best lamb
    c. the covenant box
    d. his sword

(Over)

15. Who was Bathsheba?
    - a. Jonathan's wife
    - b. Samuel's wife
    - c. Saul's wife
    - d. Uriah's wife

16. Who was Nathan?
    - a. a prophet
    - b. Saul's son
    - c. David's grandson
    - d. a priest and Samuel's son

17. Solomon was known for his:
    - a. Wisdom
    - b. Construction of the Temple
    - c. Diplomacy
    - d. All of the above

18. An example of Solomon's wisdom is:
    - a. His conquests
    - b. His use of his people
    - c. His settlement of a child's parenthood dispute
    - d. His settlement of a trade dispute

19. Where did Solomon get his workers to help build the temple?
    - a. Egypt
    - b. Syria
    - c. Romans
    - d. Drafting his own citizens

20. How did Solomon impress the Queen of Sheba?
    - a. Wisdom
    - b. His palace
    - c. His gifts to her
    - d. All of the above

21. Solomon fell away from God by:
    - a. Being greedy
    - b. Treating his workers harshly
    - c. Building a temple to several gods
    - d. Losing battles

22. Parable means:
    - a. pair
    - b. mint
    - c. an ancient song
    - d. a short story with a moral lesson

23. Tribute means:
    - a. revenge
    - b. tax
    - c. an ancient song
    - d. small hill

(Over)

24. - 33. <u>Matching Exercise</u>

____ 1. Jesus   a. a model of faithfulness to God

____ 2. Samuel   b. traditional enemy of the Israelites

____ 3. Saul   c. the wise king

____ 4. Jonathan   d. the last of the judges and a prophet

____ 5. David   e. the most famous descendant of the House of David

____ 6. Philistines   f. "They look at outward appearance, but I look at the heart."

____ 7. Nathan   g. became jealous of David's military success and his popularity

____ 8. God   h. a model of friendship

____ 9. Adonijah   i. the prophet who anointed Solomon as king

____10. Solomon   j. son of David who lost the throne

I have neither given nor received any assistance on this quiz.

_____
Signature   Date

Name: _____   Date: _____

Chapters 31-36: Samuel, Saul, David & Solomon Quiz

Please identify each speaker of the following quotes:

1. "Choose one of your men to fight me. If he wins and kills me, we will be your slaves, but if I win and kill him, you will be our slaves."

   Goliath

2. "I have killed lions and bears, and I will do the same to this heathen Philistine, who has defied the army of the living God."

   David

3. "You are right, and I am wrong. You have been so good to me, while I have done such wrong to you! How often does someone catch an enemy and then let him go away unharmed?"

   Saul

5. Samuel is…
   a. **the last of the great judges**   c. Saul's successor
   b. Israel's first king   d. Joshua's son

6. Which of the following was <u>not</u> a reason the Israelites wanted a king?
   a. To unite the twelve tribes of Israel for military protection
   b. To keep all the Israelite tribes faithful to God's covenant and Ten Commandments
   c. To defend Israel from attacks by other nations such as the Philistines
   d. **To raise money for a temple**

7. Which of the following was <u>not</u> one of Samuel's warnings about how a king might treat the Israelites?
   a. A king will make soldiers of your sons.
   b. A king will make your sons plow his fields.
   c. A king will make your daughters work as his cooks.
   d. **A king will impose taxes on trade.**

(Over)

8. What was God's theme in selecting Saul and David?
    a. Membership in the best tribes was important.
    b. Membership in the best families was important.
    c. The smallest and least appealing was important, too.
    d. Appearance was important.

9. Why did Saul present David with Michal for marriage?
    a. He was to be David's servant.
    b. He was to be one of David's officers in the military.
    c. She was to be David's servant.
    d. He planned to use her to trap David into fighting the Philistines and hopefully die in battle.

10. Who was Jonathan?
    a. Saul's son-in-law
    b. A close friend of David's
    c. Samuel's son
    d. Ahimelech's son

11. Why was David unable to kill Saul?
    a. Because he could not catch him
    b. Because Saul outnumbered him
    c. Because Saul was still God's chosen king
    d. Because Saul was stronger

12. Which of the following is not a reason to select Jerusalem as the capital of Israel:
    a. A great conquest/victory.
    b. Jerusalem did not belong to any of the 12 tribes of Israel.
    c. The selection of Jerusalem did not favor any of the 12 tribes.
    d. Jerusalem was ideally located between the northern and southern tribes of Israel.

13. How did David's men infiltrate Jerusalem?
    a. His men disguised themselves as traders.
    b. His men hid in nearby fields until nighttime.
    c. His men entered through the water tunnel.
    d. His men hid in scattered houses in Jerusalem until the time of attack.

14. What sacred object did David bring to Jerusalem?
    a. an altar
    b. his best lamb
    c. the covenant box
    d. his sword

(Over)

15. Who was Bathsheba?
    - a. Jonathan's wife
    - b. Samuel's wife
    - c. Saul's wife
    - **d. Uriah's wife**

16. Who was Nathan?
    - **a. a prophet**
    - b. Saul's son
    - c. David's grandson
    - d. a priest and Samuel's son

17. Solomon was known for his:
    - a. Wisdom
    - b. Construction of the Temple
    - c. Diplomacy
    - **d. All of the above**

18. An example of Solomon's wisdom is:
    - a. His conquests
    - b. His use of his people
    - **c. His settlement of a child's parenthood dispute**
    - d. His settlement of a trade dispute

19. Where did Solomon get his workers to help build the temple?
    - a. Egypt
    - b. Syria
    - c. Romans
    - **d. Forcing his own citizens**

20. How did Solomon impress the Queen of Sheba?
    - a. Wisdom
    - b. His palace
    - c. His gifts to her
    - **d. All of the above**

21. Solomon fell away from God by:
    - a. Being greedy
    - b. Treating his workers harshly
    - **c. Building a temple to several gods**
    - d. Losing battles

22. Parable means:
    - a. pair
    - b. mint
    - c. an ancient song
    - **d. a short story with a moral lesson**

23. Tribute means:
    - a. revenge
    - **b. tax**
    - c. an ancient song
    - d. small hill

(Over)

24. - 33. <u>Matching Exercise</u>

__e__ 1. Jesus a. a model of faithfulness to God
__d__ 2. Samuel. b. traditional enemy of the Israelites
__g__ 3. Saul c. the wise king
__h__ 4. Jonathan d. the last of the judges and a prophet
__a__ 5. David e. the most famous descendant of the House of David
__b__ 6. Philistines f. "They look at outward appearance, but I look at the heart."
__i__ 7. Nathan g. became jealous of David's military success and his popularity
__f__ 8. God h. a model of friendship
__j__ 9. Adonijah i. the prophet who anointed Solomon as king
__c__ 10. Solomon j. son of David who lost the throne

I have neither given nor received any assistance on this quiz.

_____

Signature   Date

Chapter 37: Esther

Supplemental Notes

1. The Book of Esther celebrates the courage and determination of Esther and Mordecai.

2. While Esther is a fictional character, King Xerxes, also known as Ahasuerus, did rule the Persian Empire 486-464 BCE. He also fought the Greeks unsuccessfully at Thermopylae and Salamis in 480 BCE.

Name: _____ Date: _____

Chapter 37: Esther

1. Who were the five main characters in this book and what was their position?

    a. _____

    b. _____

    c. _____

    d. _____

    e. _____

2. Who revealed the plot to assassinate the king? _____

3. Why was Haman upset with Mordecai?

    _____

    _____

4. What did Haman convince the king to do? Why?

    _____

    _____

5. What did Mordecai say to Esther to prompt her to act when she thought there was nothing she could do?

    _____

    _____

6. What custom of the king frustrated Queen Esther?

    _____

    _____

(Over)

7. Describe how the queen first tried to convince the king to save the Jews.

   _____

   _____

   _____

   _____

   _____

   _____

   _____

   _____

8. Since the king could not change his proclamation ordering the execution of all the Jews on the thirteenth day of the twelfth month of Adar, what did he do?

   _____

   _____

9. Why was the proclamation to execute the Jews not followed?

   _____

   _____

   _____

   _____

   _____

   _____

   _____

   _____

10. What is the Festival of Purim?

    _____

    _____

Name: _____   Date: _____

Chapter 37: Esther

1. Who were the five main characters in this book and what was their position? (See Ch. 37 story, p. 178-179)

    a. **King Xerxes, the king of Persia**

    b. **Mordecai, the cousin of Esther who raised her**

    c. **Esther, the queen of Persia**

    d. **Vashti, the estranged wife of King Xerxes**

    e. **Haman, the King's prime minister**

2. Who revealed the plot to assassinate the king? (Esther 2:21-22) **Mordecai**

3. Why was Haman upset with Mordecai? (Esther 3:2)

    Mordecai refused to bow and kneel before Haman as he had been ordered to.

4. What did Haman convince the king to do? Why? (Esther 3:8-9)

    He convinced the king to issue a proclamation to put to death a certain race of people (Jews) who do not obey the laws of the empire.

5. What did Mordecai say to Esther to prompt her to act when she thought there was nothing she could do? (Esther 4:13)

    "Don't imagine that you are safer than any other Jew because you are in the royal palace." (Esther 4:13) (GNT)

6. What custom of the king frustrated Queen Esther? (Esther 4:10-11)

    No one could see the king without being summoned, including the queen. If someone did, the person must die.

(Over)

7. Describe how the queen first tried to convince the king to save the Jews. (Esther 5-7)

    Esther put on her royal robes and stood at the outer edge of the inner courtyard facing the king inside. When he saw Queen Esther, he asked what she wanted. She replied that she would like him and Haman to be her guests at a banquet that night. At her banquet she invited them to come the next evening as her guests at another banquet. Then she told the king what she wanted. She asked that she and her people may live for they have been sold for slaughter by Haman. The king ordered Haman to be hanged.

8. Since the king could not change his proclamation ordering the execution of all the Jews on the thirteenth day of the twelfth month of Adar, what did he do? (Esther 8:7-8)

    He told Esther and Mordecai that they could write the Jews whatever they wanted in his name and stamp it with the royal seal.

9. Why was the proclamation to execute the Jews not followed? (Esther 9:2-5)

    Mordecai dictated a decree to the governors, administrators, and officials in all of the 127 provinces in the empire that permitted the Jews to organize for their own self-defense. If they were attacked, they could fight back, kill their attackers, and take their possessions. On the day chosen for their destruction the Jews attacked their enemies and destroyed them over that day and the next one. In fact, the governors, administrators, and officials helped the Jews because they knew Mordecai was now a powerful official in the king's court.

10. What is the Festival of Purim? (Esther 9:20-32)

    The Festival of Purim observes two days as holidays to celebrate the Jews' deliverance from Haman's planned slaughter.

Vocabulary

#	Chapter	Word	Definition
1	1	mammoth	large extinct elephant
2	1	bison	buffalo
3	1	derogatory	insulting
4	1	afterlife	life after death
5	1	hunter-gatherer	people who hunt animals and gather wild plants for food
6	1	domesticate	train wild animals and plants
7	1	polytheism	belief in many gods
8	1	drought	long spell of dry weather
9	1	pestilence	swiftly spreading disease
10	1	attribute	explain or give credit
11	1	monotheism	belief in one God
12	2	BCE	Before the Common Era
13	2	phenomenon	observable event
14	2	sect	religious group
15	3	geography	study of the physical & cultural features of an area
16	3	topography	physical features of the earth
17	3	CE	Common Era (also known as A.D., in the year of the Lord)
18	3	prehistory	period before the development of writing in 3,000 BCE
19	3	cuneiform	one of 600 wedge-shaped characters in Sumerian writing
20	3	irrigation	supplying dry lands with water by canals & pipes
21	3	ziggurat	a rectangular, stepped tower with an altar at the top
22	3	code	an organized set of laws
23	3	hieroglyphics	Egyptian writing system
24	3	papyrus	a long, thin reed; paper-like writing material
25	3	delta	a triangle-shaped area of land made of soil deposited by a river
26	3	agrarian	farming
27	3	Semitic	peoples of southwest Asia
28	3	evolution	progression
29	3	exodus	departure
30	3	famine	a terrible shortage of food that can cause starvation
31	3	fertile	productive
32	4	ford	a place where a stream may be crossed by wading
33	4	switchback	a zigzag road for climbing a steep grade
34	4	cultural diffusion	the spread of ideas, values and inventions of one culture to another

35	5	proverb	familiar saying
36	5	prophesy	prediction
37	5	testament	covenant
38	5	covenant	a solemn agreement between two parties
39	5	exile	banishment; required to leave one's homeland
40	5	messiah	the hoped-for person who would free the Israelites
41	5	scripture	religious writing
42	5	oral tradition	passed down by word of mouth from generation to generation
43	5	epistle	letter
44	5	monastery	a house for people in a religious order (e.g., monks)
45	5	canon	church law
46	6	patriarch	respected founder
47	6	genesis	origin, beginning
48	6	artifact	handmade objects
49	6	pestilence	swiftly spreading disease
50	6	calamity	misfortune
51	6	chaotic	a confused, unorganized state
52	7	salvation	to be saved, for example for everlasting life
53	7	desolate	deserted
54	7	engulfed	enclosed
55	7	resemble	be like
56	8	nostrils	nose
57	8	Eden	delight or garden of God
58	8	cultivate	grow crops
59	8	cunning	tricky
60	9	inherit	receive
61	9	scowl	an angry, wrinkled facial expression
62	10	ark	a huge boat
63	13	concubine	a woman who is not a wife but holds a recognized position in the household
64	13	circumcise	to cut off the foreskin on a penis
65	13	hospitality	a friendly and generous reception
66	13	polygamy	the practice of having more than one wife or husband at a time
67	14	ram	a male sheep
68	14	appeasement	the act of pacifying or buying off
69	15	trough	a long shallow open box-like container to feed or water animals
70	15	fodder	a course dry food, such as corn stalks, for livestock
71	16	lentil	bean soup
72	17	vow	solemn promise

73	17	tithe	to give one-tenth usually in support of a church
74	17	idol	statue or image worshipped as a representation of a god
75	18	sheaf	a bundle of stalks
76	18	cistern	a dry well; a tank or large pottery jar for storing water
77	18	caravan	a group of travelers
78	19	pharaoh	an Egyptian king
79	20	scorch	to dry or shrivel in the heat
80	20	devour	to eat greedily
81	21	guarantee	promise to pay if the product or service is not done
82	22	divination	using omens or magic powers to tell the future
83	22	maxim	principle
84	24	embalm	to treat a corpse with preservatives to prevent decay
85	24	retribution	revenge, retaliation
86	25	midwife	a woman who helps with childbirth
87	25	concoct	made up
88	26	prophet	one who speaks divinely
89	26	plague	an outbreak of disease
90	26	gnat	a very small flying bug
91	26	boil	pus
92	26	hail	small lumps of ice
93	26	sprig	small plant shoot or twig
94	26	hyssop	mint
95	26	lintel	horizontal board above a door
96	26	leavened	made with yeast; rises
97	27	chariot	Two-wheeled, horse-drawn vehicle used in ancient times
98	27	quail	a small game bird
99	27	manna	bread (miraculously supplied to the Israelites)
100	29	theocracy	a government by officials regarded as divinely inspired
101	29	avenge	take retaliation on
102	30	glean	pick up grain left behind
103	30	Gentile	a non-Israelite; non-Jew
104	31	tell	layered mounts on top of the ruins of older buildings
105	31	wean	transition from mother's milk to food; free from dependence
106	31	anoint	to apply oil in a sacred rite
107	32	harp	a musical string instrument on a triangular frame
108	34	Davidic Covenant	God's promise that David's line of descendants will endure forever
109	34	parable	a short story with a moral lesson
110	36	tribute	tax
111	37	wail	mournful cry
112	37	scepter	a royal staff used as a symbol of authority

Bibliography

Good News Bible, New York: American Bible Society, 1992.

Armento, Beverly J. et al, A Message of Ancient Days, Boston: Houghton Mifflin, 2003.

Boadt, Lawrence, Reading the Old Testament, An Introduction, New York: Paulist Press, 1984.

Break Through! The Bible for Young Catholics. Winona, MN: Saint Mary's Press, 2006.

Buehrens, John. Understanding the Bible. Boston: Beacon Press, 2003.

Burstein, Stanley M. and Shek, Richard, Ancient Civilizations through the Renaissance. Boston: Houghton Mifflin Harcourt, 2012

The Catholic Youth Bible. Winona, WI: Saint Mary's Press, 2000.

Comay, Joan. Who's Who in the Bible. New York: Wings Books, 1971.

Feiler, Bruce. Walking the Bible. New York: William Marrow, 2001.

Geoghegan, Jeffrey & Homan, Michael. The Bible for Dummies, Hoboken, N.J.: Joh Wiley & Sons, 2003

Genesis to Revelation. Nashville: Abington Press, 1997.

Gibbs Binkley, Cheryl and McKeel, Jane M., Living the Promise, Self-published with the Unitarian Church of Arlington, VA. Date unknown.

Good News Bible, Today's English Version. New York: American Bible Society, 1992.

Halley's Bible Handbook, Grand Rapids, MI: Zondervan, 2000.

Haney Schafer, Mary. The Bible & Its Influence – Teacher's Edition. New York: BLP Publishing, 2006.

Isbouts, Jean-Pierre. The Biblical World: An Illustrated Atlas, Washington, DC: National Geographic Society, 2007.

Kagan, Neil, Concise History of the World, Washington, D.C.: National Geographic Society, 2006.

Keller-Scholz, Rick & Pomanowski, Jeannie. Break Through, The Bible for Young Catholics, Teacher's Activity Manual. Winona, MN: St. Mary's Press, 2006.

Nichols, John. A Wind Swept over Waters: Reflections on 60 Favorite Bible Passages. Boston: Skinner House Books, 2007.

Pineo, Caroline, Cain's Children, A Course of Study. Philadelphia: Friends General Conference, 1970.

Reed Newland, Mary, Teaching Manual for Written on Our Hearts: The Old Testament Story of God's Love, Winona, Minn.: Saint Mary's Press, 2002

Sanders, Nancy I. Old Testament Days An Activity Guide. Chicago: Chicago Review Press, 1999.

Student Activity Workbook for Break Through. Winona, MN: St. Marty's Press, 2006.

Walker, Catherine B. Bible Workbook, Volume 1, Old Testament, Chicago: Moody Press, 1952

Williams, Derek. The Biblical Times. Grand Rapids, MI: Baker Books, 1997.

http://humanorigins.si.edu/evidence/human-fossils/species/homo-sapiens

https://religionnews.com/2017/11/16/religious-nones-are-gaining-ground-in-america-and-theyre-worried-about-the-economy-says-new-study

https://www.washingtonpost.com/opinions/even-atheists-should-read-the-bible/2018/03/30/98a1133c-3444-11e8-94fa-32d48460b955_story.html?utm_term=.15485e4052f9

https://en.wikipedia.org/wiki/History_of_male_circumcision

http://time.com/6662/the-mystery-of-the-bibles-phantom-camels/

https://news.nationalgeographic.com/news/2014/02/140210-domesticated-camels-israel-bible-archaeology-science/

https://en.wikipedia.org/wiki/Joseph_and_the_Amazing_Technicolor_Dreamcoat.

http://www.crystalinks.com/egyptdreamscrying.html

http://www.ancient-origins.net/myths-legends/egyptian-dream-book-001621

http://dreamhawk.com/dream-encyclopedia/egyptian-dream-beliefs/

http://www.pbs.org/mythsandheroes/myths_four_sheba.html

www.ingramcontent.com/pod-product-compliance
Lightning Source LLC
Chambersburg PA
CBHW080848020526
44118CB00037B/2311